THE GOSPEL CONSPIRACY
IN THE EPISCOPAL CHURCH

MICHAEL MARSHALL

The Gospel Conspiracy
in the
Episcopal Church

The Revelation of God
The Renewal of the Church
The Reformation of Society

MOREHOUSE PUBLISHING
Harrisburg, PA • Wilton, CT

Copyright © 1986 by Michael Marshall

Morehouse Publishing
Editorial Office
78 Danbury Road
Wilton, CT 06897
Corporate Office
P.O. Box 1321
Harrisburg, PA 17105

Library of Congress Cataloguing-in-Publication Data

Marshall, Michael, 1936–
The gospel conspiracy in the Episcopal church.

1. Church renewal—Episcopal Church. 2. Episcopal
Church—Doctrines. 3. Anglican Communion—Doctrines.
I. Title.
BX5930.2.M37   1986   283   86-8659
ISBN 0–8192–1386–1

All Biblical quotations (unless otherwise indicated)
are from the Revised Standard Version of the Bible,
Old Testament Section, Copyright 1952; New Tes-
tament Section, First Edition, Copyright 1946;
Second Edition © 1971 by Division of Christian
Education of the National Council of Church of
Christ in the United States of America.

Printed in the United States of America
Fourth Printing, 1990

Dedicated to

The Reverend Edward Salmon and the congregation
of St. Michael and St. George, St. Louis, Missouri
who initiated and nurtured the Anglican Institute:
for their vision, their generosity,
and their loving and continuing commitment.

Contents

INTRODUCTION

This book is not a report of the conference held in Winter Park
in January, 1986. It is a book that instead comes straight out of
the spirit engendered at that conference. It was a remarkable
occasion and those who were present, and whose names can be
seen after the open letter printed in this book, came from many
different backgrounds of renewal in the church. We were con-
scious almost from the moment the conference began that the
Lord was moving among us. "Empires" were surrendered to his
lordship and egos tamed by the gentle yet firm, overriding presence of the Holy Spirit—that special spirit of unity. We were
experiencing from the outset what the Rev. Dr. Jim Packer called,
so appropriately—"the convergence of the saints."

Yet there are few things more infuriating than for someone
to return from a holiday or some great experience in his life armed
with slides, photographs, audio and video tapes demanding to sit
down and tell his story—whose burden seems to be from start to
finish, "Oh, you should have been there!" Secondhand enthusiasm seldom catches fire.

So this book has to stand up in its own right. It was written
swiftly, immediately following the conference. You do not even
need to know that there *was* a conference in Winter Park in order
to read this book. The author hopes that this book will itself

engender in the reader something of the vision, the challenge, and the joy we all experienced at that conference. This is not a book about renewal: it is my earnest prayer that it is itself a renewing book.

But because this was written so swiftly there are two prices at least that have to be paid. The first is that there is a note of hurried impatience throughout the book. There are many undeveloped arguments and many rough edges. The author's tendency to exaggeration will annoy and irritate some readers. The trouble is that I have been to the mountain top, you see, and I have caught a vision. I have rushed down, somewhat out of breath, and I do not want just to tell you what I have seen—not even armed with the help of those audio and video tapes. Rather, I want you to see it for yourself. Frankly, it was the only way I could write this kind of book. We caught a vision at that conference, but never mind the conference! It is the vision that matters. For the vision is for our church—the Episcopal church—so come and see it for yourself. That and nothing less is the presumption and claim behind this book. God is doing great things in his church. Have you heard? Have you seen? Even if you disagree with some details here, you cannot afford to miss such a sight as may be visible in these pages for yourself.

Then the second price that has to be paid is quite simply self-evident and yet needs to be admitted at the outset. Although this book comes out of the spirit of that Winter Park conference, it is not an agreed report. There will be many things which my friends and colleagues who were present at that conference will not agree with in detail in this book. I have acknowledged in some chapters specific debts to specific speakers because much of the content of those chapters is derived from their very important presentations. Yet here again, I must take responsibility for the thoughts expressed throughout those chapters, which may or may not be adhered to in every detail by those who helped to inspire what is written.

THE CONVERGENCE OF THE SAINTS

Yet what must be said, first to last in this book, is that God is renewing his church, calling out leaders from varying traditions of renewal in our church to a point of convergence, agreement, and unified witness. That is what we saw at the conference. It is that unified witness which this book seeks to affirm, to declare, and to celebrate. As we draw to the end of the century (and happily at the beginning of a new term of office in the ministry of our new Presiding Bishop) it is evident for those with eyes to see that God is working his purpose out. He is giving to his church new strengths and new responsibilities; a new vision for new opportunities and refreshment and healing to prepare us for new battles, even more heroic witness and inevitably new suffering and martyrdom. There can be no cheap renewal if there is to be lasting and formative renewal for our church today. The conspiracy of which the title of this book speaks is not intended in any way to be either insidious or a clandestine affair. It is an open secret—open for those who are ready to open their minds afresh.

The ground base of the conference was scored in three notes: the *revelation* of God; the *renewal* of the church; and the *reformation* of society. Each of these three notes is interwoven and interdependent. The other many and varied themes arose out of and return to those three notes. Those three notes are basic to the concerns of the church for our day. We believe that they set an agenda for our church in the closing years of this century. Yet we cannot have any one of them without the other two. Strangely, truth is apparently as trinitarian as love.

The end product of all this was not so much a statement, although there was produced an open letter acclaimed by all present carrying the signatures of all members of the conference. The real end product of the conference was an experience—we experienced what we were talking about. So deep was that experience that we all returned to our own countries and our own geographies of renewal by "another way."

For in the end, there was no end product! The conference was and is part of a process. This book is also part of that same process and will in its turn further that process. Published at the same time as this book, there is a study book written by the Rev. Charles Irish, national co-ordinator of Episcopal Renewal Ministries. It is entitled *The Gospel Conspiracy Workbook*. It is our earnest hope that these two books in conjunction will energize

groups and parishes throughout America to convene around the
experience of renewal. It is that experience which in its turn will
motivate Christians and parishes to join in that same convergence
of the saints: one, holy, catholic, and apostolic church, obedient
to revelation; renewed for witness and energized for mission and
evangelism.

January 25, 1986
The Conversion of St. Paul   + Michael Marshall

ACKNOWLEDGMENTS

The author wishes to express deep gratitude to a whole team of people who helped to make this book possible at such short notice: his colleagues in renewal ministry at the Winter Park Conference, Florida; Stephen Wilburn for his patient editing which went well beyond the bounds of duty; The Reverend Charles Bewick, who acted as "wordsmith" of the conference. The whole manuscript was typed at great speed by Mary Baddeley in succession to all the other manuscripts and books she has made possible over many years. Sally Barrett completed the work with swift and expert proofreading. To all, thank you.

THE GOSPEL CONSPIRACY
IN THE EPISCOPAL CHURCH

ONE

What Is Renewal?

Renewal, in one shape or another, has been around long enough in the churches to have become something of a "has-been." Perhaps a cynic might be forgiven for concluding that the most tired word in contemporary church vocabulary, and itself a word most in need of renewal is the word renewal!

Nor is it much better to try to salvage the word by ceasing to speak of it in the abstract and then going on to attach it as an adjective to that other, equally dangerous word throughout history—movement. The renewal movement. So often in the history of the church, the one thing you can be certain of about any movement is that by the time it has become recognized and given the title of a movement—it is no longer moving! Rather, it has become a party, taking up a position on various issues. Such movements soon acquire a proper structure, constitution, and jargon, with labels and slogans. They hold frequent conferences in their own name and set themselves up against the rest of the church, as the ideal (and eventually the idol) of what a truly "renewed" church should be like. Good Lord, deliver us! Yet against such cynicism (healthy at its best) many Christians throughout the churches today would want to testify to the powerful movement of renewal that has been sweeping across the face of all the churches for the last quarter of a century. They would want to testify to this not only in their own lives but also in the lives of many churches of differing traditions. In fact, like it or not, with us or in spite of us—God is renewing his church.

As you might expect, this renewal is closely associated with the work and power of the Holy Spirit: that same Holy Spirit who was most in evidence when it all began nearly two thousand years ago at the first Pentecost. Men and women of all Christian persuasions have come to experience this Holy Spirit, not just as a theological idea to help them to "talk up" their doctrine of the Trinity. Rather, as at that first Pentecost, ideas, plans, essays and reports have all alike been overtaken and refashioned by an experience of the Holy Spirit. It is that experience which is the base line of all else that follows, tuning our theology, our preaching, and our teaching until every aspect of what we would like to call our Christian life becomes a witness to this overriding experience: the impact of the Holy Spirit. In theory we could call it by a thousand and one different names. In practice we tend to refer to it with the shorthand word—renewal.

WHAT RENEWAL IS, AND WHAT RENEWAL IS NOT

Perhaps at the outset, it might not be such a bad thing if we were to seek to define our terms by trying to state again something of what we mean, or perhaps what we should mean, when we use this word—renewal.

It has of course very little whatever to do with doing something new. "Bishop, we've got the new hymnal. We've got renewal in our parish!" No. Renewal has nothing whatever to do with novelty for novelty's sake. In fact those who have experienced this renewal in their Christian discipleship are frequently people who subsequently recover and re-express their traditional faith more faithfully and more patiently. They often discover that things which they supposed had been "cast down,"[1] are in practice and in experience being "raised up." What had grown old, is, by the work of the Holy Spirit, "being made new." It is what we have passed by (on the other side, so often) and regarded as past, finished, and dead—it is these very corpses which the breath of

the Holy Spirit infuses. We soon find ourselves with Ezekiel convinced that where once there was only death—behold, now there
is indeed new life. We witness to the raising up of a mighty army
where there had formally been a valley of dead bones.

Yet in no sense is renewal, at its best, a reaction. It is not
(nor should it ever be) an invitation to look back with nostalgia
over our shoulders—to the so called, "good old days." Those who
like to bewail the state of the church today should be sternly
recalled to a proper perspective of the church in history. The
good old days have never existed. For there are two heresies to do
with time—and they are both mistaken. The first supposes that
things must get better all the time and therefore that today's
church (always referred to by such people as modern or contemporary) is inevitably more enlightened and informed and better
than yesterday's church simply because of the passing of time. A
modern view is better, simply and solely because it is modern.
Such is a naive view of history and a pathetic view of life. It leads
to the cult of what one writer calls the cult of the neophiliacs[2]—
the lovers of some new thing. Yet the second heresy, which is
perhaps more prevalent in the church, is the view that something
is better because it is old and because the history of the church
is where "the ages of faith are to be found."

Yet in practice both views are incorrect and indefensible. The
church has always been in a mess, precisely the same mess as its
members are in. After all, its membership consists of a bunch of
forgiven sinners who have certainly not yet made it. Such a
church (like the Christian life of the individual disciple) is in
constant need of reform and renewal. For the church (and again
this is exactly so for every individual disciple within it) needs
renewal each and every day for precisely the same reason as I need
to make my bed every morning when I get out of it. It has been
used and now it needs making again. Yesterday's manna (in the
Old Testament story of the feeding of God's people in the desert)[3]
is no good today. It has to be gathered afresh, with dependency
each and every day of our pilgrimage. "New every morning is the
love" writes that apostle of renewal in the nineteenth century,
John Keble. And he is right.

So we need a theology of renewal and at the same time a renewal of theology. We need a theology of renewal—what it is and what it is not. It is not revival. Well, it is not revival if you mean by revival (what presumably the word literally means), coming back to life. Jesus did not come back to life. Jesus died and Jesus was raised by the power of the Father. That is the thrust of all apostolic preaching in the New Testament. Jesus did not come back to life; Lazarus did, but then there is no good news to do with Lazarus. Pood old Lazarus! Lazarus's revival was tearful and pitiful. So is revival. It means we just have to try harder and try to beat it up and make it happen all over again! There is something about revivalist church life that has tended to be abrasive, aggressive, and rooted in *our* energies and *our* enthusiasms. There is a real difference of chemistry between renewal and revival. We should not pray for the revival of the church. We have been that way many times before and it has always led to a new rigidity, more ecclesiasticism and (like all revolution) to a new tyranny.

Neither should we pray for the survival of the church. Jesus did not go on living after death; he did not survive the grave. He was not some sort of superstar or superman who was stronger than death. In every sense he was raised by the power of the Father. Survival means presumably having some kind of intrinsic immortality—the ability to go on going on in spite of everything. Jesus did not go on going on. He underwent his Passion and his Death. He was then raised up by the power of the Father. In the very earliest account of the meaning of Christ's death, Paul explicitly produces a kind of four point manifesto; possibly even *reproducing* one that was current among the Christians of his day. It runs as follows: Jesus died for our sins; he was buried; he *was* raised on the third day; he appeared to his disciples. That, and nothing less than that, is the four point formula the early church proclaimed as the essence of its doctrine of the resurrection of Jesus.[4]

Furthermore it was this formula that was preached by the apostolic church. It became abbreviated into a neat and slick slogan that summed up the whole content and point of their preaching: "Jesus and the resurrection."[5] So much did these two points belong together in a single reality that some people thought

Paul was talking about Jesus and someone else who was called "resurrection!" So much did the two belong together—this Jesus and his resurrection—that you might have been forgiven for supposing that resurrection was the name of an affair that Jesus was having with his church. (Perhaps that is not such a bad doctrine of the church, after all!)

THE RENEWAL OF THE CHURCH AND THE RESURRECTION OF JESUS

We can go further still. Perhaps resurrection is very much what we mean by renewal in the church, for Jesus and the resurrection became for the early church not so much a mandate but more a whole way of life. Jesus (and his resurrection) was the very life of the early church in those days immediately following Pentecost. For the Holy Spirit was sent as Jesus had promised his weak and worried disciples that he would be sent. And when he was sent, he did what Jesus promised he would do. He took the things concerning Jesus (his life, passion, death, and resurrection) and made them present, vivid, and formative in the lives of those disciples.[6] The events of Jesus's life, passion, death, and resurrection were no longer events from the past that needed to be remembered with nostalgia, taking the disciples backward down memory lane, "to the good old days when Jesus used to . . ." "Do you remember the times when he used to . . .?" That sort of conversation was presumably the constant theme of the bewildered and beleaguered disciples in those paralyzing days between the resurrection and the Pentecost. They were locked in a type of fortress, going over "the snapshots" and the "tape recordings" of the good old days. When, however, the Holy Spirit came at Pentecost they were "released" from the prisonhouse of past, fond memories, and far from sticking to the past, suddenly they found that these past events were beginning to stick to them. These events were beginning to take over their whole way of seeing life. They were being shaped by the very events of the passion, death, and resurrection of Jesus.

This was now the way they began to see the whole of life.

Furthermore, the works that he did, they were now doing, as he
promised—"and even greater works."[7] The blind were seeing, the
deaf were hearing, the lame were walking, the dead were being
raised up, and even the poor were hearing the good news. It
worked! Jesus (and the resurrection) was at work in their lives
and in their world. It was to become a whole new way of seeing
the whole world. "He is not dead; he is alive" and he reigns. This
is the new regime of thought breaking into the world. It is called
the Kingdom of God. The dying and rising of Jesus was itself the
very formula and chemistry of the messenger who preached this
message. The message and the messengers had the same features
and profile: it was always the profile of Jesus and the resurrection.

So those early preachers of the gospel did not see the messengers as a separate organization set up to spread the message,
as a sort of ecclesiastical marketing board! They did not think of
the church (themselves) as a kind of organization which they were
trying to run effectively along good management lines in the hope
that the sale of the gospel product would increase each year. The
message and the messengers were two sides of one and the same
coin. The catholic church (as people would call it now) was the
embodiment of the gospel and the gospel was at the same time
the representation (always in flesh and blood terms, and not in
the abstract) of the dying and rising of Jesus. Life, truth, and
reality were Jesus-shaped, and Jesus is that same Jesus who suffered, died, was buried, and was raised and who now kept ap-
pearing (it was almost as though he was coming out of the
woodwork) in the life of the church. It was happening everywhere: the blind were seeing, the deaf were hearing, the lame
were walking, and even the poor were being enriched with the
good news and . . . (wait for it!) the dead were being "raised."
There it is. The new life of resurrection was at work in the lives
of tired, weary, broken men and women. So Archbishop Michael
Ramsey writes:

> The mistake of ecclesiasticism through the ages has been to
> believe in the church as a kind of thing-in-itself. The Apos-
> tles never regarded the church as a thing-in-itself. Their

faith was in God, who had raised Jesus from the dead, and they knew the power of his resurrection to be at work in them and in their fellow believers despite the unworthiness of them all. That is always the nature of true belief in the church. It is a laying hold on the power of the resurrection."[8]

That is "the nature of true belief in the church" and we could add that it is also the nature of a true understanding of what we really mean by renewal. Renewal is a laying hold on the power of the Resurrection. Renewal, which becomes a "thing-in-itself," will rapidly degenerate into a new triumphalism and a new (or rather jaded) ecclesiasticism. Of course, Christians love the church. But they must love it first because Jesus loves it and gave his life for it. And they must love it most when it talks most of Jesus, and uplifts, raises, and glorifies Him by its words and by its deeds.

For that is why the Holy Spirit comes—to glorify Jesus. "Yet the Holy Spirit had not been given, because Jesus was not yet glorified."[9] A church which only glorifies itself and seeks to raise itself up for its own glory—to such a church the Holy Spirit will not be given. The church glorifies and raises up Jesus: Jesus glorifies the Father who has and does raise him up continually.

So renewal occurs, like resurrection, when, either individually as Christian disciples or as the church corporately, we are made like, and conformed ever more deeply into the likeness of, the death and resurrection of Jesus. Renewal occurs when that message in its turn forms the life of the disciple in such a way that that life itself becomes a sign of life through death, the experience of power in powerlessness, the receiving of riches in the very midst of our poverty—in fact all the signs of gospel contradiction. In a word, renewal is conformity to the likeness of Jesus in his death and in his resurrection. It is probably most vividly experienced and most evident at those points of weakness and breakdown in our own life. It could be that those who prophesy the death of the church for example are in reality (albeit in their ignorance) strange heralds of renewal. For it is precisely at those moments when we know ourselves to be most at our weakest—it is those very moments when we can become closest to

receiving God's own strength. To be brought to our knees is a
very good posture indeed! For, when we are finished, then God
can begin. We can be lifted up and carried best when we struggle
least. Those are the moments and the places in the history of the
church when renewal is most in evidence. So look out when
people begin to talk about the death of the church.

For renewal is not something that we can do at all. There is
no agenda of things that we can do in order to "get renewed." A
little like the rich young ruler in the New Testament, renewal can
be the latest thing we have heard of, as he had recently heard
about "eternal life." So he asks "what must I do to *get* eternal
life?"[10] We can be tempted together with him by our acquisitive
outlook to ask, "what must we do to get renewal?" There is nothing that we can do in ourselves to acquire this illusive characteristic.

THE RENEWAL OF THE CHURCH AND THE
TRANSFIGURATION OF JESUS

Renewal is what God has done and is doing in his servant Jesus,
whom we have crucified and whom we continue to crucify. Yet it
is this same Jesus whom God has raised and who appears to us
continually. The church is particularly apostolic when it witnesses
in its own life (and death) to the power of that resurrection. That
was the only real qualification in the book of the Acts of the
Apostles for the choice of the twelfth apostle in the place of
Judas—he must be a witness of resurrection. That is the only
qualification for a truly apostolic church. It must continually witness to the death and resurrection of Jesus Christ. And, furthermore, it witnesses best not only in the message which it preaches,
but rather when the lives of those same messengers (the church)
are themselves signs and sacraments of that message. When the
church (as a bunch of messengers as well as a pile of bricks) is
cruciform in shape, then it is renewed. Its appearance, its image,
and its countenance are all changed as surely as the face of Jesus
was changed on the mountain of transfiguration.[11]

In some ways we should speak of the renewal of the church

as the transfiguration of the church. It is sad, though perhaps ironical, that many New Testament scholars should speak of the story of the transfiguration in the New Testament as "a misplaced resurrection appearance." In fact it occurs in all three of the Gospels (as does very little else) and always at one of the important turning points in the ministry and life of Jesus. However, suppose it is a sort of misplaced resurrection appearance. Perhaps that also is not such a bad description of the church!

But suppose also that it really did occur when the Evangelists say it occurred—on the road to the crucifixion—then perhaps it will help us understand better and recapture the vision of renewal for the church more clearly if we locate the transfiguration of Jesus where the Evangelists insist it occurred. In the story of the transfiguration of Jesus as told by all three synoptic Evangelists, we are led from Peter's witness to Jesus as the Christ at Caesarea Philippi, to transfiguration, to revelation and from there down the mountainside to ministry and involvement in the world. All three accounts, though varying in detail, present this block of material as shaped essentially in the way that we have just described: revelation, renewal, reformation. Peter's confession or witness must open him (unless he is to be satanic) to the reality of suffering. There is no cheap proclamation of orthodox faith. Faith in Jesus and witnessing to Jesus demand the willingness to be broken. Even truth is cruciform in shape: it is not a straightforward line, and it is certainly not (as in other world religions) a circle. It is a cross and Peter has to go a long way yet before he can begin to see things in that way: crucified and upside down. Yet that is the shape of things to come, Peter, and therefore it is no accident that the word in Greek for witness, *martureo*, is also the same word that gives us the word for martyr in English. So Jesus is right: "Beware when all men speak well of you."[12] Beware when the church's teaching and its confession of faith are popular. That sort of gospel, like much therapeutic religion or success-oriented preaching today, always ends up where Peter very nearly did (very, very nearly did)—straight up and on the side of Satan!

So we need even now, at this stage of the journey, to see the full shape of things to come in the event of the transfiguration.

There the Holy Spirit *overshadows*[13] the little apostolic band as
they enter the cloud and all their self-assurance for the moment
is gone. They were afraid as they entered that cloud: a "cloud of
unknowing." As they fell on their faces, Jesus is raised up as Lord
of the law and the prophets (speaking with Moses and Elijah),
and so begins to show to his disciples the point of it all: the
exodus he is about to achieve in Jerusalem. The face of Jesus, his
image, is changed. He is transfigured. So will his church—if it
will pursue this way and make this event the essential event of
its life and its identity.

It is out of this experience of faith, witness, suffering, and
transfiguration that an authoritative and powerful ministry is
born. There is no self-fulfilled path to authentic and powerful
ministry: that road begins with costly commitment and confession
of faith in Jesus. Only so are we raised up with him by the Father
and plunged into the passion of his compassion, his ministry, and
his healing. If that is what we mean by renewal, it will have very
little indeed to do with triumphalism or ecclesiasticism and everything to do with Jesus and his love both for his Father and for
the world. And that is the only sort of renewal which, in its turn,
has the power to renew. The shape is trinitarian: revelation
(Peter's confession);[14] renewal (the transfiguration of Christ); and
the reformation of society (ministry, mission, and witness).

And all this God is doing again in our generation, and we
are witnesses of these things. In our day we are privileged to
witness once again to the mighty acts of the God and Father of
our Lord Jesus Christ who is once again raising up Jesus in his
Body—the church. "It is the Lord's doing and it is marvelous in
our eyes."[15] It is Resurrection from the dead, as surely now as it
was then. The test of orthodoxy now is the same as it was then—
Jesus came in the flesh—and therefore his resurrection is in the
flesh,[16] the only flesh he has, namely, ours. That is the ultimate
joke. That is the ultimate miracle and the ultimate absurd contradiction. All the narrative of the scriptures from the first pages
of Genesis through the incredible stories of the history of Israel,
through prophets and wisdom literature have led up to this ultimate contradiction. Now we can ask with eyes open, staring in

amazement, and with the same incredulity as was experienced by Mary in her words when she first asked: "How on earth can this be?"[17] How can flesh and blood carry and bear within it the holiness of God? The reply to us at all points in the history of the church will be the same as the reply to Mary in that once and for all annunciation: "The Holy Spirit will come upon you and the power of the Most High will overshadow you; therefore the child to be born will be called holy"[18]—and his name is always Jesus. Jesus, God's final and fullest word to us; Jesus, God's word to us of good news; Jesus and the Resurrection.

Wherever that word is preached and proclaimed; wherever that word is received, marked, learned, and inwardly digested;[19] wherever that word is celebrated with thanksgiving and eucharist; wherever that word is loved and cherished and obeyed; wherever there is space for that word to rest and abide in the heart of the believer[20]—there is always resurrection and renewal. And it is always the Lord's doing. It is his loving initiative, who, when he saw us cast down, raised us up together with his servant Jesus. "Without God we cannot," said St. Augustine, "without us he will not." There is the paradox of our redemption, our renewal, and our resurrection.

In retrospect, however, for those with eyes to see, and perhaps even in prospect for those who have the discernment to read the signs of the times, it is no accident that such renewal should break into our story at this point in the history of the church of God, especially in the West. For in spite of itself the church has been ripe for renewal for several decades, but now in these last fifteen years of the second millennium, and with the same urgency as always accompanies the alarm clock of Advent, "now is the accepted time."[21] "The day is at hand and the night is far spent."

Before we analyze in detail the proper response and obedience of the churches, for which this gift of resurrection and renewal calls, we need to analyze the present state of the churches, and especially the Episcopal church in the United States. We shall find initially a disturbing quantity of bad news. Yet as always it is precisely among the garbage of the bad news that we find the good news. Frederick Buechner writes: "The gospel is bad news before it is good news."[22] Freed by God's grace from aggression, arrogance, pride, or party strife, or that most deadly of perversions of zeal—ecclesiastical neurosis—we need to look how far we have fallen from that first love for Jesus and his resurrection. Only then, with confidence in God and the sufficiency of his grace alone, can we lay hold on what he is doing in our day and seek to make it our own with simplicity of spirit and deep gratitude of heart and mind.

Notes

1. Prayer by Archbishop William Laud.
2. Christopher Booker, *The Neophiliacs* (London: Fontana/Collins, 1969).
3. Exodus 16:19–20.
4. 1 Corinthians 15:3–8.
5. Acts 17:18.
6. John 14:26; John 16:14.
7. John 14:12.
8. A. M. Ramsey, Michael Ramsey, Leon-Joseph Suenens, *The Future of the Christian Church* (Morehouse-Barlow Co., 1970), p. 38.
9. John 7:39.
10. Matthew 19:16.
11. Luke 9:29.
12. Luke 6:26.
13. Luke 9:34.
14. Matthew 16:17.
15. Psalms 118:23.
16. 1 John 4:2f. and 2 John 7.
17. Luke 1:34.
18. Luke 1:35.
19. Proper 28, *Book of Common Prayer.*
20. See John 8:32.
21. Romans 13:12.
22. Frederick Buechner, *Telling the Truth* (New York: Harper & Row, 1977), p. 7.

TWO

The God of Resurrection and Contradiction

THE GOD WHO ACTS

"The gospel is bad news before it is good news" (Frederick Buechner). Certainly when the church seeks its own ends and its own strength there is only bad news. Whenever the church tries to tailor its message to fit comfortably into the prevailing climate of the contemporary world view of the day—in a word when the church is secularized—there also there is only bad news. If Emmanuel, God with us, is good news, we can always be certain that mankind without God, however idealistic and loving we may seem to be, always is bad news.

Nevertheless, bitterness about the state of the church or cynical party strife within the church can have no real place in church renewal. The devil is quick to seize even the good wine of renewal and turn it sour whenever the advocates of renewal seek to set themselves up as in any sense "the real church." Leaders in the renewal world make an ugly picture if they dare to believe, even for a moment, that somehow renewal produces a superior, elite type of Christian, raised up to recall the church to its true identity. True renewal seeks only to raise up and to lift up Jesus, to glorify him: "I, if I be lifted up," said Jesus, "will draw all men to myself."[1] And so in any conference of renewal or in any concern for renewal, there must be a constant reminder of the Christ-centered nature of true renewal. It is only such a constant re-minder that saves renewal from becoming a new party in the church, destroyed by pride and divisive in spirit.

Furthermore, there can enter into the best of our concerns for God's church an unhealthy ecclesiastical neurosis which falls into the snare of believing that unless we rush forward to prop up the church, it will fall and be destroyed. There is that ugly title to a book on the renewal of the church, by Andrew Greeley, *How to Save the Catholic Church.*[2] That is really a very nasty title, indeed. It smacks of just that same neurosis (to say nothing of pride) that persuaded Uzzah to rush forward to stop the ark from falling from the cart, when the ark of the Lord was being moved to Jerusalem at the orders of David.[3] As soon as Uzzah touched the ark (admittedly with the best intentions in the world) he was struck dead. Uzzah, perhaps, needs to become the patron saint of all renewal leaders (Fr. Greeley included) to save them from precisely that presumption and neurosis which would lead us to imagine that by some special knowledge (gnosis) or some special insights, special programs—gestures, vestures, or postures—the church will be renewed and saved. If God did not spare his own son, he is not going to spare his own church from all the vicis-situdes of living in a sinful and fallen world. Yet he is faithful (as he was to his son Jesus) and will at the last raise up Jesus and together with him all those who are being saved.

Albeit at the same time we sound such a warning against misplaced zeal and neurosis, there is a real need to read the signs of the times and to discern the spirit of unbelief in our church today. It is not so much that the church does not believe in God. That would indeed be a false accusation. But it is rather that the church in many areas of its life today apparently no longer believes in a *God who acts.* God has become an idea rather than an event, and so our whole theology (our knowledge of God) and our spir-ituality (the way we try to live out that knowledge) lacks any sense of expectation. There is no room to be surprised—not even by joy. The contemporary church faced with the question of John the Baptist to Jesus, "Are you he who is to come or shall we look

O God, the Father of Jesus, by your Holy Spirit you have set your Church to be the sign and instrument of your Community of love, justice and peace. We pray for the Bishop's Conference on Christian Community; bless all who attend, especially Ken and Ruth Genge and the planning committee, that they may lead us to discover a deeper sense of our place in the Body of Christ and help us to be true Communities of Faith willing to do your work in the world.

for another?"[4] is more likely to send back an essay on Christology than to witness to the mighty acts of God in our midst whereby we also together with Jesus can recount with thanksgiving: "The blind receive their sight and the lame walk, lepers are cleansed and the deaf hear."[5]

In Old and New Testament alike, we do not come to know God by making him in our own image. The Bible is not a book about God in that sense at all. In that sense the Bible is the least religious of any of the great books of the world religions. In the Bible we only come to know God and what he is like by the way he acts. The Scriptures are the record of God's mighty acts since the beginning of time. He shows us his hand before he shows us his face. However, the ultimate and definitive act of God in Jesus and the act in which we see his mighty hand most at work is supremely the death and resurrection of Jesus Christ. So the New Testament church did not preach theism or deism and then seek to add on to that belief an extra compartment of theology around the person of Jesus, the Holy Spirit, the church, and prayer. Rather the early church started the other way round. In the New Testament we start with a proclamation which always begins with a challenge, "What think ye of Christ?"[6] It is Jesus who shows us what God is like. He is the image of God supremely in his death and resurrection. It is only this saving belief, offering the evidence of death and resurrection, which consequently convenes and constitutes the church. Theism and deism are powerless as evangelistic theology. Yet, it is theism and deism that are so characteristic of whole areas of barren life in the church today.

DEISM AND THEISM—NO EARTHLY USE

We should know (because we have been this way many times before) that always the same barren outcome issues from such a paucity of theological beliefs. The Church of England at the beginning of the eighteenth century, for example, was a church paralyzed by theism and deism. The end of the seventeenth century and the first half of the eighteenth century "was a time of scientific confidence but of social and religious confusion."[7] The

church was tired of the religious wars of the previous age and set
its face against zeal and enthusiasm. It is interesting to note not
only the decline of the Church of England at such a time, but
also how deism and theism then swept across the face of the
church. There was belief in God all right, but in a God who is
the absentee landlord of the universe, which he created and to
which he is largely indifferent. Creation is completed, static, and
the laws of nature are immutable.

In such a view of God as the watchmaker of the universe
there is no room for intervention or for a God who acts. He has
made the watch, wound it up, and left it to run while he observes
from a safe distance. Nothing could be further from the God of
the Bible from cover to cover, nor indeed from the one who has
acted and continues to act in and through the person of Jesus
Christ. It is of no small interest to observe how Robert Boyle
(1627–91), the "father of chemistry," drew up the terms of ref-
erence for the famous Boyle Lectures founded in honor of his life
and his learning. Money was left to provide for sermons, "for
proving the Christian religion against notorious infidels, namely
atheists, *theists*, pagans, Jews, and Mahometans, not descending
lower to any controversies that are among Christians themselves."[8]
What emerges from this packaging together of theists with atheists, pagans, Jews, and Mahometans is that you can clearly believe
in God and still be an "infidel," for as Scripture is not ashamed
to remind us, the devil also believes in God.[9] The God of the
deist or the theist does not act, however. He does not interfere.
We cannot come to know him through his intervening acts. We
are driven simply to a kind of natural theology as observers of the
universe in which we hope to discern something of the face of
God.

So it is not incidental that one of the early Boyle lecturers
addressed his subject in the following words:

> They [the deists] see that things generally go on in a constant
> and regular method; that the frame and order of the world
> are preserved by things being disposed and managed in a
> uniform manner; that certain causes produce certain effects

in a continuous succession, according to certain fixed laws
or rules; and from hence they conclude, very weakly and
unphilosophically, that there are in matter certain necessary
laws or powers, the result of which is that which they call
the cause of nature, which they think is impossible to be
changed or altered, and consequently there can be no such
thing as miracles. [10]

There is the bondage and legalism of the deist and the theist
in a nutshell. On the contrary however, St. Paul exhorts us, "Do
not be conformed to this world but be ye transformed by the
renewal of your mind." [11] Or we can read that same text in J. B.
Phillips' translation: "Don't let the world around you squeeze you
into its own mold." Yet such a theology as the theology of the
deist and the theist are truly trapped and squeezed into the tyranny of the thought-forms of the secular world. They leave no
room whatever for God to act within the world of matter or within
the world of the observable sciences.

We need to observe three factors that belong to this kind of
view of the universe. In the first place it must be said that it is
not a particularly scientific view. Scientists in the eighteenth century had a rigid and static view of the world of observable matter
and their "laws" emerge (at least to the layman) as immutable
and rigid. Since Darwin however, especially today in the field of
physics, there is much less scientific dogmatism abroad. Scientists
(especially geologists and biologists in recent years) seem able to
live with conflicting regimes of thought in a world of science
observed through far more dynamic doctrines and observations.

Second, the proper response to scientific triumphalism was
not for the church to retreat into a theology of the "god of the
gaps," and seek to demarcate an area of reality that was purely
spiritual and that could remain uninvaded by the scientists. It
was as though we responded to the encroachment of the scientists
into the territory of theology by withdrawing to only that territory
which could not be explained by science or in any other way. We
then proceeded to name that territory as spiritual and to put up
a sign to the scientists and to all other responsible branches of
learning that read "Hands Off." Such a view of God (as the god

of the gaps) destroyed in a single sweep of the pen any idea of
the cosmic lordship of Christ.

> He is the image of the invisible God, the first-born of all
> creation; for in him all things were created, in heaven and
> on earth, visible and invisible, whether thrones or dominions
> or principalities or authorities—*all things* were created
> through him and for him. He is before all things, and in
> him all things hold together. He is the head of the body, the
> church; he is the beginning, the first-born from the dead,
> that in everything he might be pre-eminent. For in him all
> the fulness of God was pleased to dwell.[12]

For if Jesus is not Lord of all, he is not really Lord at all. A
Christianity that proclaims the Lordship of Christ only over the
"spiritual realm" (whatever that may be) is a theology which is
far from biblical, sacramental, incarnational, or traditional. Such
a doctrine of Christ is a new gnosticism and breeds a psychology
that is little better than schizoid.

Third, theologians who have allowed themselves to be
squeezed into the mold of this kind of thinking always find the
empty tomb a real stumbling block. It is hardly surprising. If you
have given over the material world totally to the so-called laws of
nature, then the only sort of resurrection for Jesus is purely spiritual—again, whatever that might mean. The reversal of death
in the resurrection has occurred only in the spiritual realm. Matter and the body (and indeed all those things that we have made
such a mess of) are left where they apparently were and always
will be: locked in the tomb of the legalism of the laws of nature
along with the bones of Jesus somewhere in Palestine.

THE EMPTY TOMB AND APOSTOLIC CHRISTIANITY

Now that is not what Paul is proclaiming in Romans, chapter 8.
That is not the world view of the Lordship of Christ as we find
it in the Epistle to the Colossians. That is not New Testament,
full-blooded apostolic preaching. And finally, of course, that is
precisely the very opposite of what all four accounts of the res-

urrection of Jesus in the gospels are at pains to tell us. The account of the resurrection in the four gospels disagrees about many things in detail, yet strangely all four accounts are unanimous on this one point—that the tomb was empty. Indeed for all four of the Evangelists that is the starting point of the whole absurd fact of the resurrection. That was the first sign of contradiction on Easter morning. That was what the disciples had to wrestle with as they sought to make sense of a new shaped and new sort of universe that seemed to be breaking into their consciousness. Slowly they had to accommodate this whole new regime of thought as it broke into their prejudices. The world was a different shape after all. The whole world, not just the spiritual world, had to be seen now in a different way.

It is true that a full-blooded doctrine of the resurrection of Jesus is formed around a personal encounter with our risen Lord. Until that point, for all of the disciples, it was little more than a question of rumors of immortality or just gossip about an empty tomb. For, the empty tomb in itself does not produce a resurrection experience. Only a full-blooded resurrection experience can in the end convene and constitute the Catholic Church of the risen Lord. Yet, there is no full-blooded event that the Church recognizes as the resurrection of Jesus Christ without that empty tomb. There is no good news for our world if resurrection is reduced to the memory of Jesus living on in his disciples. Mozart has done that with a rather better accompaniment on the whole! Neither is there any good news in ghosts or spirits and things that go bump in the night. That is not the resurrection of Jesus Christ either. "See my hands and my feet, that it is I myself"[13] Jesus reassures his disciples then as he does now. "Handle me and see; for a spirit has not flesh and bones as you see that I have."[14] Luke wants to get the point across once and for all and so he drives it home. "And while they still disbelieved for joy, and wondered, he said to them, 'Have you anything here to eat?' They gave him a piece of broiled fish, and he took it and ate it before them."[15]

For those (sometimes in leadership positions in our church today) who find the physical resurrection of Jesus and the empty

tomb unacceptable to contemporary thought forms, and who
therefore seek to extrapolate a purely spiritual view of the resurrection, we need to say severe and important things. Such an
emasculated doctrine of the resurrection is totally opposed to the
New Testament witness of the church and its tradition. It is in
fact precisely the opposite of what the record of Scripture seeks
to convey. Furthermore, such a doctrine of a purely spiritual resurrection is not the witness of the apostolic church to the Lordship of Jesus Christ in the epistles of the New Testament, where
that resurrection was preached with power. A spiritual resurrection leaves the church powerless to address the flesh and blood
needs of our every day world. It is frankly a middle-class sophisticated gospel for middle-class sophisticated people, who neither
require nor want the lordship of Christ over matter, money, sex,
and power. They are managing very nicely in that realm, thank
you. They can go to church for purely spiritual therapy and call
upon the resurrection as evidence for feeling better after a time
of depression, but they do not want the profile and architecture
of their material world radically re-ordered by the resurrection
and by all that it implies about the nature of the kingdom of
God. If they do, it will not be according to the radical challenge
of the Resurrection of Jesus. Nor will it belong to a truly spiritual
re-fashioning of matter under the lordship of Christ. Such re-
ordering as there is will be kept safely away from the material
world and will tend to draw all its energies and formulas from
largely political ideologies.

    For the apostolic preaching of the resurrection was a sacra-
mental sign in history, in flesh and blood terms. It was a sign that
invaded matter and was spelled out in actions that spoke far louder
than words a clear message: it told the world in no uncertain
terms that matter matters to God. Matter matters to God just as
much in redemption as it does in creation. As John Polkinghorne,
formerly professor of mathematical physics at Cambridge, England, now ordained as an Anglican priest, writes:

    If we believe that the tomb was empty, as I do, certain con-
    sequences follow . . . one thing that the empty tomb says to

me is that matter has a destiny, a transformed and transmuted destiny, no doubt, but a destiny nevertheless. The material creation is not a transient, even mistaken episode. Of course that is a deeply mysterious thought.[16]

"Behold, I tell you a mystery" says St. Paul as he expounds the apostolic witness to Resurrection. 'We shall not all die, but we shall all be *changed*.'[17] That radical transformation of the universe, as the new regime of thought (which we call the kingdom of God) breaks finally and irreversibly into history, time, matter, and the world of the senses—this new regime promises to be traumatic, but never emasculated or thinner than the world of the senses that we now experience. The kingdom will not be less material in form. It is more substantial than even matter itself. It makes large stones look like styrofoam on a stage set. The stone in Palestine is easily moved by the breaking dawn of the kingdom. The doors of our resistance are easily penetrated by the more substantial reality of God's love breaking through and refusing to be excluded by fear. We cannot explain how the matter of our everyday lives will indeed be reordered into this wider and richer environment of the spirit, but the New Testament refuses to let it be discarded. "Gather up the fragments that remain that nothing be lost"[18] is a sign of the resurrection in John's gospel. Such a sign refuses to leave bones scattered and discarded around Palestine as irrelevant to the evidence of the resurrection preached by the apostles. Yet preaching that seeks to ignore the empty tomb (if it is any longer worthy of the word preaching) was inevitable in the deism and theism of the eighteenth century and is current once again in our own age. Such an emasculated gospel (if it is any longer worthy of the word) is powerless to change people's lives. It reverts to moralism at best and puts goodness in place of holiness, education in the place of salvation, enlightenment in the place of repentance, and therapy in the place of salvation. In a word it empties pews. That is what it did in the Church of England in the eighteenth century, and that is what it has done and is continuing to do in parts of the Episcopal church and the Anglican churches throughout the world in the twentieth century. But thanks be to God, he will not suffer his church to be pulled down in this way any more than he "will suffer his Holy One to see corruption."[19]

For God is working his purpose out and will vindicate the resurrection of Jesus in his church wherever there are men and women who can say with Mary, and by God's grace: Amen: so be it. The church is intended to be the Amen to God's promises. And so in every generation whenever we have crucified Jesus by our faithlessness, our arrogance, and our weakness of mind, this same Jesus whom we crucify, God raises up. It is there and then that renewal begins. It always begins in the hearts and lives of a few. This renewal is so bound into history, time, place, and matter that it even has a geography in the lives of men and women. Their friendships seem to overlap and form communities and convergences. It frequently comes out of conferences and shared concerns. Furthermore this renewal often picks up the name of a place where resurrection was experienced and where witness was articulated: the Oxford Movement, the Clapham Sect. Who knows, perhaps the Winter Park Conference?

Yet renewal is never just an idea like a meteorological depression wafting generally in a northeasterly direction. It has roots and a face. It even has an address and a telephone number! In the Bible we see the record of renewal in the history of the old Israel; there and then as here and now, it has a pattern and substantial features. The many are saved by the few; the few are saved by the one. "There went with him a band of men and women whose hearts God has touched."[20] The apostolic band always strikes up a few bars among a few people but the theme is always the same—Jesus and the resurrection. Without that, "we are of all men (and women) to be pitied most."[21] A church that is not convened around witness to Jesus and his resurrection is as miserable as an English Sunday, all dressed up and nowhere to go!

ANGLICANISM AND RENEWAL

So in each generation (for renewal is not something you can ever say you've got once and for all) God raises up Jesus and together with him an apostolic band. In the blight of the church, which had surrendered to deism and theism in the eighteenth century, God raised up the three great W's—Whitefield, Wesley, and Wilberforce. Their lives and their friendships overlapped not only chronologically but even geographically. Wesley, who spans in a long lifetime almost the whole of the eighteenth century (1703–91), knew Whitefield and worked with him, and Whitefield in his turn influenced Wilberforce not least by a crucial letter that he wrote to him and that spoke to Wilberforce so eloquently at a moment of crisis. (Letters have always been a part of apostolic witness, it seems.) These three men spell out the fulness of the gospel of Jesus and the resurrection in the three evidences that characterize Anglicanism: Scripture, sacrament, and service.

Whitefield was a man of the Scriptures and therefore a man who preached with power. He was an evangelist and an apostolic witness out on the road, traveling and preaching in season and out of season. There is no renewal in the church where there is not the experience of powerful and apostolic preaching by the evangelist. Come back, evangelists; all is forgiven!

Then there was John Wesley, that great Anglican preacher and teacher. He also was a man of the Scriptures; he also traveled (extensively), and he also had a gospel to proclaim. But he had more. It is often said that Whitefield left behind him a trail of fireworks, which soon burned out. It was Wesley however who left behind him groups and bands and classes of men and women (largely from among the poor). They lived the life of the gospel and yet as the poor who had been made rich by God's grace appropriated by faith. In other words, Wesley planted churches as a visible, sacramental, and tangible expression of hearts touched and set on fire by the word of God. He saw that the structured church is indeed a sign of the gospel.

Third, there was the witness of William Wilberforce—the politician who was responsible for the abolition of the slave trade and for passing a bill to that effect through the English Parliament. At one point he thought he should be ordained to the priesthood but was advised to remain a layman committed to changing the architecture of the English economy and of English

society in the eighteenth century. All three of these men together
spelled out God's answer to the death of the church in eighteenth-
century England. They embodied the fullness and richness of a
Gospel that was firmly built upon the foundations of Scripture,
Sacraments, and service; seen another way, as built upon the
foundations of word, worship, and works. At heart, it is the Anglican threefold formula of Scripture, tradition, and reason, those
rich ingredients of a full gospel casserole that so constitute the
chemistry of Anglicanism at its richest and fullest.

That was the good news in the midst of the bad news in
England in the eighteenth century. And it is God's word: it is
his first word and it is his last word. And that word is Jesus and
the resurrection. It is renewal and furthermore it is not past history. It is an ever-present possibility and our eternal hope. What
God did to renew his church in the eighteenth century is happening again in our own age and in our midst. The Winter Park
Conference, of which to some extent this book is the record,
witnesses to that same power of God at work in our weakness as
surely as he was at work in the death and resurrection of Jesus.
Our confidence throughout the conference was based on nothing
else—we were determined to know only Jesus and him crucified,
and not to turn to any other substitute or any other gospel ("not
that there is another gospel"). [22] The conference was both an event
and an experience. It was so much more than just words. It was
the overlapping of lives and of friendships, set in a particular
geography with a name, an address, and a telephone number. We
were all enormously aware that the Lord was doing great things
for us and among us already. Renewal became for us just that—
God in our midst. It was as though we touched, handled and saw
his power at work in our weakness and his new life at work in
the death of his church. "It was (for it always is) the Lord's doing
and it is marvelous in our eyes."

Notes

1. John 12:32.
2. Andrew Greeley and Mary Greeley Durkin, *How To Save the Catholic Church* (New York: Viking, 1984).
3. 2 Samuel 6:3ff.
4. Matthew 11:3.
5. Matthew 11:5.
6. Matthew 22:42.
7. David Holloway, *The Church of England: Where Is It Going?* (Eastbourne: Kingsway Publications, 1985), p. 71.
8. Ibid.
9. James 2:19.
10. Samuel Clarke, *Boyle Lecture 1704.*
11. Romans 12:2.
12. Colossians 1:15ff.
13. Luke 24:39a.
14. Luke 24:39b.
15. Luke 24:41ff.
16. John Polkinghorne, *The Way the World Is* (SPCK, 1983), p. 86.
17. 1 Corinthians 15:51.
18. John 6:12.
19. Acts 13:37.
20. 1 Samuel 10:26.
21. 1 Corinthians 15:19.
22. Galatians 1:7.

THREE

What on Earth Is Happening in the Church Today?

DISCERNING THE BODY

God is doing something new in his church today, and we need to stop and see it if we can read the signs of the times. For things are not quite what they used to be. The old badges and slogans no longer signify the same differences. Old party lines no longer represent what they did. In fact wherever renewal is at work throughout the churches, there are new cleavages but at the same time new points of convergence. All this can be very confusing. Nevertheless, all this demands a new sense of thankfulness as well as a new plea for discernment. We certainly need, in St. Paul's phrase, to "discern the body"[1] of Christ. The old divisions are passing away and new ones are now occurring in different places on our map. Although this process is happening across all the churches worldwide, the particular concern of this book is to seek an assessment of what is happening in the Anglican fellowship of churches worldwide and what is happening in the English-speaking part of that fellowship in particular.

In the nineteenth century, renewal issued in a cleavage be-

For the content of much of this and the following chapter the author is indebted to a lecture given by the Rev. Prof. J.I. Packer at the Winter Park Conference.

tween the catholic renewal movement on the one hand, which began in Oxford around the person of Newman in the 1830s, and the evangelical renewal of the same period, which focused around the person of Charles Simeon and the church in that rival university, Cambridge. Much of the catholic renewal of the Oxford Movement was perceived as Neo-Romanism. It was easily recognizable by Tridentine coloring and was assessed and eventually damned in the eyes of the evangelicals in the ritualistic movement that issued out of Oxford a generation later in the externals of "vesture, gesture, and posture." It appeared that the two renewed and revitalized groups in Anglicanism, Evangelical and Catholic, were implacably condemned to polarize. Witness was seen over and against worship, the word over and against the sacraments. Evangelicals stood in one corner and catholics were spoiling for a fight in the opposing corner.

In the second half of the twentieth century, although there is still a cleavage in the church, it is along very different lines from those in the nineteenth century. Today, the cleavage is between Christians who hold to the trinitarian faith on the one hand as opposed to a form of Anglican unitarianism on the other hand. The cleavage is between a full-blooded apostolic Christianity rooted in the historical reality of the incarnation on the one hand, as opposed to another view that would see Jesus Christ as little more than a special case of the indwelling of a man with the spirit of God. It is between a view of Christ as first and foremost the divine savior as opposed to Jesus the model of religion and the good life. While there are still those who insist upon the bodily resurrection of Jesus as an actual historical event, showing up in the spectrum of matter, time, and history, there are others for whom the risen Christ is essentially a powerful memory of a formative personality who has influenced the course of history. That memory now invites "disciples" to model their lives upon his surviving and continuing spirit at work in the world and the lives of those disciples. In a word, the cleavage is between a religion that is God-given or man-made; between a religion primarily of revelation, and a religion of speculation.

It is when you see this cleavage as the basic one for our age that you also see a realignment of the old parties. Things are no longer what they seemed to be. We have all ended up with some strange bedfellows. You will find for example catholic Anglicans and evangelical Anglicans converging and uniting on both sides of this new cleavage. But what will probably amaze you more than anything is that (for the want of a better phrase) it is those Christians from both parties (evangelicals and catholics) who in some sense and at some point have come under the influence of the renewal movement who find themselves standing together on the same side of the new divide. Many of the old slogans and issues that seemed to divide them in the past have been literally transcended. They have struck out from behind the barricades of well-dug theological trenches and have converged now as allies at a point beyond which their former traditions had led them.

Today many basic doctrines are no longer a matter for dispute between evangelical and catholic Anglicans. Justification by faith is established and basic for both groups as God's last judgment, and furthermore that judgment is one of acquittal because of the saving death of Jesus. Because that judgment is in some sense eschatological, we experience our justification and can speak of our salvation as something that is established in God's providence and the fruits of which we are beginning to enjoy even now here on earth and in time. There is a new confidence in the power and authority of Scripture. Furthermore, the old polarization between witness and worship has been transcended. Both former parties are ready to affirm that true witness leads us into worship, and worship inevitably involves witness—that witness, which is compelled to testify in the words of the book of the Acts of the Apostles, "We cannot but tell what we have seen and heard."[2] Both groups describe salvation history as ruin, redemption, and regeneration.

Such is the nature of this convergence. It is a convergence of doctrine and theology but a kind of theology that is perhaps best described as spirituality: theology as experiencing God. It is a new richness and a new plenitude to which this convergence witnesses and it is calling out all those involved to go further along the converging lines of two formerly irreconcilable traditions.

THE WORK OF THE HOLY SPIRIT

And all this would be acknowledged as a result of a new and deepening experience of the Holy Spirit. It is so often the Holy Spirit who in his dynamism takes what has been static and atrophied and by both breaking it up and linking it up, *re-forms* the body. Put another way, and once again for the want of a better word, the old parties have come under the influence of the charismatic movement. They may not have all become as individuals card-carrying charismatics, yet the formalism and rigidity of the two main blocks within earlier chapters of Anglican Christianity are, praise God, passing away. This is the work of the Holy Spirit to form and re-form, by his own gentle overshadowing, the body of Christ. As we sing at Pentecost:

> What is rigid, gently bend;
> What is frozen, warmly tend;
> Straighten what goes erringly.[3]

Or as Metropolitan Ignatios of Latakia said at the ecumenical council of churches in Uppsala in 1968:

> Without the Holy Spirit,
> God is far away,
> Christ stays in the past,
> The gospel is a dead letter,
> The church is simply an organization,
> Authority a matter of domination
> Mission a matter of propaganda
> The liturgy no more than an evocation
> Christian living a slave morality.

> But in the Holy Spirit:

> The cosmos is resurrected and groans with
> The birth pangs of the Kingdom.
> The risen Christ is there,
> The gospel is the power of life
> The church shows forth the life of the Trinity
> Authority is a liberating service
> Mission is a pentecost

The liturgy is both memorial and anticipation
Human action is deified.[4]

Of course we can all tell all sorts of horror stories from our experience of the charismatic movement. We know all too well of congregations divided by its influence. We know that judgmental spirit that draws lines between first- and second-class Christians. We know of a mindless charismatic enthusiasm that has more to do with hysteria than holiness. We are aware of the dust bowls where the ground of faith has been torn up by strife, pride, arrogance, and party spirit within congregations. Yet surely, throughout history, the passions of renewal are most evident first of all when they kick up the dust and have a scrap; it is only later when the dust has finally settled, that we begin to see those same old truths in a new light. In a sense, we have to admit that the church must choose between two sets of problems. We can have a church (a little like the church in Corinth perhaps) that is untidy, exuberant, and overflowing with life. Or we can have a nice tidy graveyard where the grass is cut and not a voice is heard because everybody is dead!

SPIRIT AND STRUCTURE: FREEDOM AND FORMALISM

So then, two cheers, perhaps, for the charismatic movement. For the truth is that the Spirit needs the structure and the structure needs the Spirit. The structure (like the bones in Ezekiel) without the Spirit rapidly degenerates into rigidity and formalism. The catholic cardiac condition that sets in by the third and fourth generation of every catholic renewal, and that was so in evidence by the beginning of this century, had to be seen to be believed. It was a case of reverting to formalism and legalism. For "today's freedom will become tomorrow's institution"[5] and it is the "institutional or structural reduction of ecclesiology" that was challenged by the charismatic movement. Praise God!

Yet at the same time the Spirit needs the structure. For the Spirit forms the body, and the Holy Spirit forms the body of Christ. The Holy Spirit, like lightning, needs grounding if it is not to burn us up. Spiritual experiences that are not directed and grounded into structural power soon degenerate into subjectivism and mere enthusiasm. Fire and water (Christ's baptism of water and the Spirit) certainly produces steam, but steam needs harnessing if it is to have the power of real movement. So with the charismatic movement, which, if left to itself, is frankly little more than steam left to itself. It has often been more evident as frenetic activity than as directed and controlled power. For it has to be admitted that the structures of the church had degenerated into formalism (both in the evangelical and catholic movements). They were crying out for a breath of fresh air and a spark of new life—nothing less than a new pentecost. At the same time, we need to be aware that whenever the charismatic movement has been left to itself, historically it has broken away from the institutional church and the sacramental structures in the name of freedom of the spirit and soon found itself doing little more than "shaking one set of structures in order to prepare for another one."[6] Spontaneity has an unpleasant habit of running into a new formalism. In practice it was not long before even the charismatic movement, so evidently a movement of freedom in the spirit, had degenerated into slogans and jargon; even this movement soon took up its own particular "gestures, vestures, and postures!"

"Perhaps it is time for us to realize that as long as we debate institutions and structures, and not the mystery of the church in her depths, we are by-passing the real issue."[7] It is to that very debate and above all to that experience of the mystery of the church in her depths that the charismatic movement, at its best, has led both evangelical and catholic Anglicans. Our first task is to lay hold of this God-given convergence and to discern it so that we can recognize it and celebrate it.

All true renewal begins with vision. "In the year that King Uzziah died, I saw the Lord of hosts."[8] For Isaiah that year, that date, and that place (the temple) marked the beginning of eighth-century renewal in Judaism. Vision leads us to true repentance and there is no unity for the church without that repentance. So many "schemes" of unity in the institutional church seek to take institutional blocks of unrepentant Christian churches and join them up. They tackle this process with fine intentions, but they begin without vision and they seek to continue without repentance. Such schemes have very little to do with that unity of the Spirit of which the New Testament speaks. They are not witnessing to the process of unity but struggling to achieve institutional *joinery*; little wonder they come unglued and fall apart so often at the seams.

Unity in the Spirit demands both vision and repentance. If we take our Isaiah model seriously, we discover that vision is a very disturbing gift. Little wonder that Jesus in the New Testament asks the blind man what he would like Jesus to do for him.[9] It is not so obvious as at first it might seem: "Do you really want to see?" Vision can be painful. "O God, I see!" may be a cry of joy or a cry of sad and sudden realization. "Now I see. There it was staring me in the face and I was too blind to see it." There really is a convergence of the saints occurring at the present time throughout all the churches, but until we see it, discern it, celebrate it, and receive it, and make it our own with thanksgiving, we could go on blindly repeating all the old slogans, digging the old trenches even deeper, remain blind as to the location of our real allies (and by implication), unaware also of the location of our true enemies.

Yet vision in its turn issues in repentance, that glorious New Testament word, perhaps the most dynamic word in the whole Christian vocabulary. Repentance means a new insight issuing in a new outlook. It means a second thought issuing in new priorities and a new direction (which in turn open up new perspectives). In a word, it is a pretty shattering experience. "The foundations of the temple were shaken at the voice of him who called."[10] Yes, the foundations of the church are intended continually and in each generation to be shaken afresh by the word of God. When Mary in the New Testament had her vision of the angel of the Annunciation, Luke reports that she was greatly troubled.[11] The French would use the phrase *boul versé*. Head over heels. Lovers experience it and according to the New Testament so did those who heard the first apostolic preaching in the book of the Acts of the Apostles. It literally turned their world upside down.[12]

For it is only through the experience of repentance that we can enter upon true renewal, a brave new world of new perspectives. At the conference at Winter Park in 1986 there were many forebodings concerning the wisdom of bringing together so many men and women who were conspicuous leaders of renewal because, quite frankly, as one observer put it: "So many people together and all of them with egos the size of a house in one place and at one time." That was asking for disaster! And so it was, humanly speaking. All kinds of empires and territorial assertions might have meant that there was no place for movement or realignment. Yet what saved the day at that conference is what saves the day in the church at large: vision and repentance. From the first evening when Dr. Packer used the phrase "convergence of the saints" eyes were opened, scales fell from our eyes. There was recognition. Those words rang true. "Now I see" the convergence of the saints. That is what God is doing in his church. Some were shaken, some were initially cautious, but all in some sense repented. The very attendance at the conference by busy people at a busy time at short notice meant that things were literally worth a second thought in the minds of those who had taken the trouble to attend. If we had not given it a second thought we would probably not have been there. So there were moments of real celebration at that conference because there was true repentance.

THE RENEWAL OF THEOLOGY

All of this was rooted in deep foundations—foundations of theology—a theology of renewal, but also a renewal of theology. So often renewal movements have been mindless movements of enthusiasm, carried away by every blast and wind of vain doctrine. There can be no lasting renewal in the church without both a theology of renewal and also a renewal of theology. Repentance, new insight issuing into a new outlook, is the very *heart* of real theology. But here we are speaking of what one writer calls "theology as doxology." Here we are rescuing the word theology from the dusty debates of distracted professors and placing it back where it belongs, at the heart of the people of God. Here we are speaking of theology as spirituality, as the experience of God, for theology is for godliness if it is to be formative in the life of God's people. Theology, Archbishop Anthony Bloom reminds us, is not knowing about God; even less is it knowing what other people have written about God. Theology is the knowledge of God. It is, therefore, awesome and like matrimony should not be undertaken by any lightly or wantonly, but soberly, discreetly, and in the fear of God. For there is a right fear of God in all the processes of theology: that same fear of God that the Bible regards as the beginning of wisdom.

Such theology must never be mindless, but at the same time it must refuse to be imprisoned by the intellect. The anointing spirit in Isaiah Chapter 61 releases captives and those who are bound. We must pray for our theologians. We must pray that theologians who are frequently captives of rigid and chained cerebral processes, and imprisoned within ideas, issues, and formulas, may be released. The age of reason and the enthronement of the intellect soon pass away, as they are indeed doing, but of course sometimes in their turn they bring the opposite extreme: a quest for mindless and mind-blowing experiences. A plague on both these houses. For there is a yet more excellent way. It is the way that we are bidden to pray by the eastern mystic, Bishop Theophan. "Stand before God," he tells us, "with your head in your heart." Often the charismatic release to which so many Christians today can testify is a release and opening of doors which have been locked between head and heart.

It is interesting to note in the discipleship of that great Anglican Christian apologist, C. S. Lewis, the development in his own theological understanding of pain. In 1940 he wrote (primarily with the mind) *The Problem of Pain*. It is a remarkable and deeply theological treatise on the contradiction and paradox of pain in a world created by a God who loves us. But it was 21 years later, in 1961, when he wrote (presumably from experience in the heart, the experience of bereavement) *A Grief Observed*. There is the theology of discipleship: theology as spirituality, theology as experiencing God.

And that is the kind of theological renewal many of us experienced at the Winter Park Conference in 1986. That is the
theological renewal we need in our church in general and in our
seminaries in particular: a theology of heart and mind. In a word,
we need a theology of structures that leaves room for the spirit.
At the end of the day, when you have sought to order and define
your theology of the Spirit (as indeed we must) there must still
be room for God to have the last word. It often comes (like the
punch line of a joke) to help you to see the point of it all. It
reminds us, as Faber once wrote so powerfully:

> For the love of God is broader than the measures of man's mind,
> And the heart of the eternal is most wonderfully kind.[13]

Only a rich theology of the Holy Spirit will give us a rich
theology of the church. Let us face the blunt facts. Much of our
theology of the church is concerned with the church as an institution, and furthermore as an institution largely shaped and fashioned by the structures, models, and patterns of the society which
that Church seeks to serve. For example, it is hard to speak of
bishops and episcopacy without seeing it as a package deal: prelacy, hierarchy, and frankly medieval prince bishops or nineteenth-
century members of the English House of Lords. Classical ecclesiology is rife with "structures, institution, and legalism and the
product of confessional polemics, of the great Western crisis of
reformation—counter-reformation."[14] But today we do not have to
burden episcopacy with all of that. Our theological language need
not always be burdened by that historical and sociological baggage. We can, if we want, contemplate with mind and heart "the
mystery of the church in her depths."[15] That is the work of a
theology of the Holy Spirit.

As the church emerges from the kind of institutionalism necessarily envisaged by Richard Hooker in the seventeenth century,
it can begin to unpack that baggage. In the seventeenth century
to be an Englishman and to be a member of the Church of
England were regarded as synonymous. But by the close of the
twentieth century we can discern a church that is increasingly
recognizable as a church of the book of the Acts of the Apostles.
That does not mean that we have to be trapped again into sup-

posing that nothing which is not recorded in the New Testament
as part of the life of the apostolic church can be countenanced
in the life of the church today. That is bondage and imprisonment
indeed. But at the same time, like a good cook, we can taste and
test the casserole to see whether we recognize the recipe and even
the aroma as that which mother used to cook so memorably in
days past. After all, in science and creation, nothing is capable
of renewing anything except the force that first created it. So
with the church. You can polish up the brass of the institution
forever and still not recapture the aroma of the mystery of that
apostolic church with its powerful and fruitful witness.

THEOLOGY OF THE HOLY SPIRIT

Let there be no mistake. Our challenge to the church is a theological challenge in the sense in which we have defined theology.
You can only afford to have a high doctrine of the church if you
first have a high doctrine of the Holy Spirit. Furthermore, by very
definition a theology of the Holy Spirit is necessarily more pre-
carious than most other doctrines in Christian theology. For the
Holy Spirit does not draw attention to himself and is therefore
somewhat more illusive. His very work and nature is to rescue us
from the idolatry of tidy formulas and neat edges. We need to
remember that all doctrines in the church are at best only signposts, like poles at the side of a highway after a snow storm. They
are intended to keep you on the road and out of the ditch. At
best all doctrine of the church must be secondary to the experience of the church. *Lex orandi:lex credendi.* It is as the church has
prayed and worshipped and experienced the Holy Spirit over
hundreds of years that it has been led to make creedal statements.
Experience leads to and generates the doctrine: the doctrines in
themselves are powerless to lead us or to generate within us the
experience. It is one of the great hallmarks of Anglicanism that
unlike many churches that were influenced by the Reformation
we are not a confessional church. That is to say, you cannot turn
up a confessional statement anywhere and say positively and precisely "Here is Anglicanism." We are a church that derives its
identity from worship as outlined and formulated in a prayer book.
That is healthy.

So we shall need to come to our work of the doctrine of the Holy Spirit without the limitations of secular education. Like those wise men of old, our education in theology will displace us from secular presuppositions where we may feel at home. We will become pilgrims and disciples out on the road. Our theology will not be done just in libraries and faculty rooms on a diet of claret and polished conversation. Our food for the journey will be God's word, our conversation in that heaven toward which we press. Our education and all our exploration will culminate not in the idolatry of dead formulas, but in worship and adoration, with heads bowed and hearts on fire. That is what we mean by a theology of the church and the Holy Spirit and that is what all true theology must always be—nothing less than doxology.

Notes

1. 1 Corinthians 11:29.
2. Acts 4:20.
3. From "Come, Thou Holy Paraclete," *The English Hymnal,* No. 155.
4. *Main Theme Address* in the Uppsala Report 1968 (Geneva, 1969), p. 298.
5. A. Schmemann, *On Mariology in Orthodoxy* in Marian Library Studies, 1 (1970), pp. 25–32.
6. Ibid.
7. Ibid.
8. Isaiah 6:1.
9. Luke 18:41.
10. Isaiah 6:4.
11. Luke 1:29.
12. Acts 17:6.
13. Frederick William Faber, "There's a wideness in God's mercy," *The Hymnal 1982,* No. 469.
14. See A. Schmemann, op. cit.
15. Ibid.

FOUR

Renewal and the Dynamic of the Spirit

STRENGTHS AND WEAKNESSES

> Not that I have already obtained this or am already perfect;
> but I press on to make it my own, because Christ Jesus has
> made me his own. Brethren, I do not consider that I have
> made it my own; but one thing I do, forgetting what lies
> behind and straining forward to what lies ahead, I press on
> toward the goal for the prize of the upward call of God in
> Christ Jesus. Let those of us who are mature be thus minded;
> and if in anything you are otherwise minded, God will reveal
> that also to you. Only let us hold true to what we have
> attained.[1]

There is the agenda. "Let us hold true to what we have at-
tained." Yes, let us recognize where God has brought us in this
process of renewal: to the convergence of the saints. As we saw
in the last chapter, that point of convergence represents a real
transcendence over past divisions, establishing many Christians
from many differing traditions on new territory, beyond where any
of those traditions in themselves could have established us. No
one tradition, valuable and important though traditions are (indeed there is no appreciation of the present without knowledge
of and faithfulness to past traditions), no one tradition has within
itself alone the richness of this further maturity.

Without forgetting our traditions, then, we need nevertheless to forget and lay aside all the slogans, badges, and jargon of our previous traditions and now strain forward to what lies ahead. That forward movement is part of the "upward call of God in Christ Jesus." Furthermore it is part of God's faithfulness to lead his people, by the Holy Spirit into the plenitude of truth.[2] Such a plenitude is assured and indeed is eschatologically already established. When the going is difficult and there are apparent setbacks, it is this hope of our calling that will keep us steady and on course, refusing to speak of either failure or success, doom, boom, or gloom, because the victory is assured and the prize is already in evidence.

That is how St. Paul could speak of the future, in spite of hardships and the apparently overwhelming size of the task. (After all, on the surface he belonged to a minute, persecuted sect; he was himself in prison at the time he was writing these words and yet pits himself against the massive power of an empire, which at that point would be regarded by most people as safely established for a thousand years.) So despite divisions within the church and between the churches, and despite a society where evil is daily at work in apparently more and more grotesque forms, we need to recover a confidence in the power of God to be at work in our powerlessness. Paul grasped that principle from the very outset in the salad days of his dealings with the beginnings of the Corinthian church. He had to recall those early Christians to the scandal of the cross. The absurdity of the cross is the power of God and the wisdom of God. There must be no new aristocracy of renewal in the church today. There must be no private sense of having been called to renewal leadership. That kind of strength and that kind of wisdom cannot do the work of God. St. Paul, we are told by Eusebius, was a little man who was bow-legged. He had a big red nose and he could not speak very well. I wonder if today he would be regarded as a spiritual leader of renewal?

Yet it is precisely through such people that God's strength is best experienced. God's strength is made perfect in our weakness. Perhaps the church, and as individuals also we have to come to the point of breakdown before God can begin to break through.

It is only when we are finished that God can help. It is so often true in history that the very point of deepest decline and of deepest darkness has been (with the benefit of hindsight) precisely the point of renewal and the moment of the dawn and the sunrise. "Shall we sin more then that grace may abound?"[3] No, certainly not. That is not a reason for the church to seek the cult of weakness and ineffectiveness nor is it a reason to glorify our stubbornness and sinfulness as disciples of Jesus Christ. It is a reason, however, to glorify in the cross of Christ Jesus and to see the contradiction of Calvary as the real (indeed, the only) basis for hope in the church.

Only when we are empty of all the spirit of self-sufficiency can we be truly filled with his own Holy Spirit. It is in those who can no longer do what they used to be able to do (for example, the very elderly like Anna and Simeon[4]) that God is free to do most. Poverty of spirit is always the first beatitude: "Blessed are those who know their need of God" (says the New English Bible translation of the more familiar phrase: "Blessed are the poor in spirit"). The church is most blessed when it knows most keenly its need of God: "And if you know how to give good gifts to your children how much more will the heavenly Father give the Holy Spirit to those who ask him."[6] And if all this is what you mean by the charismatic renewal in the church, then surely we need more and more of it. Whatever led us to suppose that we could possess anything in the life of the church in our own right or in our own strength. We do not have anything in the life of the church or indeed in life at all which is not a gift; and presumably that is all the word charismatic means. All prayer is gift; all ministry is gift; nothing is ours by achievement. Thank God, gifts are received and not achieved. So with the gift of the Holy Spirit, which is given to his church in its need, in its weakness, in its poverty, and in its emptiness. And it is only the Holy Spirit who will displace us from any complacency by driving us out (as surely as he drove Jesus out into the wilderness) beyond where we are, to where he would have us be.

We need to recall the theological nature of the work of the Holy Spirit that alone can give us those very guidelines and that important map for continuing the journey of our renewal. For unless we have about us the discontent and homesickness of pilgrims, we could be tempted to settle down now, first building booths and then very swiftly upgrading them to mansions of renewal, locking the doors, pulling out the telephone wires, and hoisting the flag of renewal on the mountain top of our fantasies. It will be the Holy Spirit alone who can drive us onward and away from these kinds of delusions. It will be the Holy Spirit alone, if we will receive his presence and his power at work in our lives, who will help us to distinguish his presence from the divisive and destructive spirits of our own limited and easily exhaustible enthusiasms. It will be the Holy Spirit alone who can rescue us from the gilded baits of triumphalism.

THE DYNAMIC OF A TRINITARIAN FAITH

The first footprint we can discern and follow in our theological pilgrimage and experience of renewal is the New Testament truth that the Holy Spirit glorifies Jesus Christ. "He will glorify me, for he will take what is mine and declare it to you."[7] Here is the heart of a truly trinitarian faith. In the dynamic of true love revealed to us in the trinity, we see the shape of things to come. In the world it is every man for himself: in the kingdom it is every man for others. "Greater love hath no man than this that a man lay down his life for his friends."[8] The greater love, the new love that is revealed to us in Jesus Christ, has the nature of trinitarian love because it never owns anything for itself and never draws attention to itself. Listen for a moment to how this is worked out in those few verses from St. John's gospel: "I have yet many things to say to you but you cannot bear them now."[9] Jesus does not need to burden us now and to tell us it all at this point. Jesus does not need to be overbearing with his disciples and crush them, not even with the truth. We can crush people even with our love and our truth! Such an overbearing disposition springs from anxiety. It is the anxiety that if I do not get this point across it will get lost. (We can sometimes see this happening in a discussion group where one part of the discussion rapidly becomes a mon-

ologue.) Yet in the dynamic love of the trinity, there is always
another who will endorse what has to be said and pick up on the
points that may fall to the ground: he is Holy Spirit. "When the
Holy Spirit of truth comes he will guide you into all truth; for he
will not speak of his own authority, but whatever he hears he will
speak."[10] The Holy Spirit is the record of truth, he sets the agenda
of love, but he is not concerned to speak of himself; he speaks
whatever he hears. In other words he is a good listener! (The very
opposite of that soloist of which we spoke earlier and who so often
dominates discussion groups.) What a blessing a good listener is
in any discussion! Two is company, three is babel. Three people
all talking and trying to tell it all soon reduce discussion to a
contest with each only concerned to make his own point. But if
one at least is listening and will only speak what he hears, that
makes all the difference in the world between heaven and hell!
So the Holy Spirit we are told will "glorify Jesus." He will spend
and be spent in drawing attention to Jesus and in making Jesus
clear and articulate. Yet even this Jesus in what he speaks and in
what he has, does not *possess* this truth, nor indeed does he
possess anything of his own or of himself, because "all that the
Father has is mine."[11] Jesus possesses nothing of himself either;
he only has this from the Father's self-emptying generosity.

Here is the new love and new life of the kingdom, imaged
and modeled on nothing less than the life of the blessed Trinity.
It is of course, sadly, the opposite of most group dynamics and
certainly the very opposite of what the world means by glory. This
self-annihilation is a vital ingredient in true love as opposed to
so much that we see in the world of self-aggrandizement parading
as love. For example, there can be much in the love of parents
for their children that is little more than self-aggrandizement;
they can so easily want the children to turn out just the way they
want as a kind of extension of themselves, bringing glory to themselves. The counterbalance and corrective to this must be something along the lines of self-annihilation, "the ability to accept
not to be, no longer to exist in a situation because something
else matters more. By this I mean the following: John the Baptist
said about himself, "I am the friend of the bridegroom." The bride

is not his bride, neither is the bridegroom his bridegroom, but such is his love for both of them that he brings them together— he is their witness and their companion in the marriage feast: he brings them to the chamber where they will meet face to face alone in a fulfilled relationship of soul and body, and he remains outside lying across the door so that no one should disturb the mystery of this love."[12]

This is the unique quality of the Holy Spirit. This is what Dr. Jim Packer calls the matchmaker ministry of the Holy Spirit. The Holy Spirit draws us to Jesus and in so doing does not draw attention to himself. He is solely concerned with making a match. So the Holy Spirit in glorifying this Jesus draws us to him in those many expressions of our love for Jesus and his love for us.

O Jesus! Shepherd, Guardian, Friend,
O Prophet, Priest, and King;
My Lord, my Life, my Way, my End,
Accept the praise I bring.[13]

Devotion, adoration, holiness of life—all these are evidence of the Holy Spirit glorifying Jesus, lifting him up, making him truly present, bringing his words to the remembrance of the one who prays. The Holy Spirit lifts Jesus up and in turn this Jesus will draw all men to himself. Indeed the test of the work of the Holy Spirit as opposed to all those other divisive spirits to which we are all too easily prey is that Jesus is more present. He becomes more real, in his words, in the fruits of the spirit which form the life of Jesus (his love, joy, and peace) and in their turn these become part of the life of the believer.

THE HOLY SPIRIT AND THE CHRISTIAN LIFE

This Holy Spirit who glorifies Jesus has what has been called a floodlight ministry. Good lighting, trained on a building, is hidden in its niches and does not draw attention to itself. Indeed you should not be able to see the lights at all. On the contrary good lighting draws our attention away from itself and is concerned only to illuminate the building, picking out every detail, showing up that detail with vivid clarity. In one sense, it shows off the building at its very best and "in the best light," as we would say. That is what the Holy Spirit does in glorifying Jesus in the church.

Second, the Holy Spirit authenticates the word of God, what John Calvin used to call "the spirit's inner witness." Indeed we cannot really read the Scriptures unless we read them in the light of the Holy Spirit. When we read the word of God, overshadowed by the spirit of God, the things of Jesus (in Old and New Testament alike) are recalled, remembered, and evoked with a vivid power in the present, and with a personal appeal that speaks directly to the heart and mind of the reader. The Holy Spirit makes Jesus an existential reality. It is as though the words we read are in italics. They spring out of the page. This was the experience of St. Augustine in the garden in the year A.D. 386: *Tolle, lege* (pick it up and read it). He picked up the Scriptures and the word of God became in that moment, Jesus: "Put on the Lord Jesus Christ."[14] This is what happened and what continually happens in the history of God's people when they read the Scriptures. Once we experience that dynamic of the Holy Spirit's work in reading Scripture, we cannot doubt that the Bible is the word of God, however many puzzles scriptural criticism may rightly present to us. We find that God is working *through* the Scriptures, making himself known through the word made flesh and wrapping the whole of salvation history around God's final and definitive word to us—Jesus. Put another way, Holy Scripture is God preaching. This word of God in Scripture, on the printed page is empowered by the Holy Spirit to speak to us. We are able to move in a single step from what the words meant when they were written to what they mean to us today. The Holy Spirit opens to us the Scriptures as surely as Jesus did to those first two disciples on the road to Emmaus.[15]

Third, the work of this Holy Spirit is discerned in the supernaturalizing of natural lives, leading us to an authentic holiness, which in practice makes possible a way of life far beyond anything we would expect as ordinary and normal. We find ourselves able to love the seemingly unlovable, not with our own love but rather with the love that Jesus Christ has for them. Even our prayer is no longer our own. "It is not you who prays," says St. Paul, "but the Holy Spirit who prays in you."[16] This is prayer in the spirit which natural man, even in his own devotional spirit, can know nothing of. It was Isaac Walton who said of Richard Sibs: "Of that good man, may just praise be given, heaven was in him, before he was in heaven."

Fourth, there is the need to recognize that the Holy Spirit creates and sustains authentic church experience. For a long time Christians (especially from the reformed traditions) tended to set the church and its life over and against the gospel and evangelism. It was precisely to counter this polarization that Michael Ramsey wrote his book *The Gospel and the Catholic Church* as long ago as 1936. "The doctrine of the church, and its order, ministry, and sacraments must not be expounded primarily in terms of an institution founded by Christ, but in terms of Christ's death and resurrection of which the one body, with its life and its order, is the expression."[17] For conversion to Jesus Christ is not a summons to be alone and to fly to the alone. God and his love have been revealed to us as trinitarian and the summons to faith is to take our place in a community, a family, a dynamic of love which we can best express in terms of membership in a body. We see this authentic church experience in the Gospels, where Jesus speaks of the new synagogue: "Where two or three are gathered together in my name, there am I in the midst."[18] Or we see again in St. Luke's gospel that witness to the risen Lord which brought the disciples together and that same risen Lord being made present in their midst.[19] And furthermore, this convention of disciples constituting the church with the adored and risen Lord in the midst of them is an effective sign itself of the gospel. The church is the environment in which the word is preached with power. Those who come into this fellowship experience the gospel and respond accordingly with repentance, forgiveness, and healing. The early church, as St. Paul does, can bear witness to the power and effectiveness of the church (that is to say disciples gathered in the fellowship of the spirit, with Jesus glorified in the midst). They will tell you, as St. Paul frequently does, that such a mix-

ture is combustive and the gospel is experienced with power.[20]
The church becomes a sign of the gospel and authenticates the
gospel to the rest of the world. Such a church is certainly not
something other than the gospel. Furthermore, out of such an
authentic church experience issues a compelling evangelism. "We
cannot but speak of what we have seen and heard." It is not long
before the gospel is unavoidably gossiped about beyond the boundaries of the church, its structures, and its buildings.

THE HOLY SPIRIT AND UNITY OF THE BODY

We then need to recognize the place of unity, which is so specially
and powerfully the work of the Holy Spirit. For the Holy Spirit
always brings together fragmented insights. In the fourth chapter
of the Epistle to the Ephesians the writer speaks of the ascended
and glorified Christ "given to each" of us separately, yet by for-
bearance held together in "the unity of the spirit in the bond of
peace." "For there is one body and one spirit"—though at the
same time there is a great diversity of gifts. For no one person
has the totality of all those gifts or a monopoly on all those
insights. There is necessarily within the body, with its diversity
of members a deep sense of interdependence and no room whatever for a sense of competition. If there is no sharing there will
be no enlarging of vision. The very word *koinonia* means precisely
that. It means literally give and take within the fellowship of
unity. The variety and rich range of gifts given by the Holy Spirit,
whenever and wherever Jesus is lifted up and raised up among his
people, equips the saints. But this is not in order that each can
build an empire, but rather "for the building up of the body of
Christ until we all attain to the unity of the faith in the knowledge of the son of God, to mature manhood, to the measure of
the stature of the fulness of Christ."[21] That is both the measure
of renewal and the challenge of unity and we must settle for
nothing less. "We are to grow up in every way into him who is
the head into Christ."[22]

Rivalry between the parts of the body has no place in the
divine scheme. Paul develops this theme and works out its full

implications in that classical passage on the interdependence of the members of the body of Christ in chapters 12 to 14 in his first Epistle to the Corinthians. "The head cannot say to the hand I have no need of you."[23] Whenever one member is tempted to play tyrant over the others, there we shall find cancer at work in the body. Take a cross-section, for example, of healthy human tissue and there you will discern diversity and interdependence at work. Cut across a cancerous growth however, and you will see how one cell has run amok and played the tyrant—the monomaniac. So within the body of Christ. Those who see a single issue with great clarity, whenever they behave as though no other insights were of any importance, then there the Spirit is quenched, there we find disunity and fragmentation. There is refreshing evidence today of the unitive work of the Holy Spirit at work in local churches. In recent years and as part of renewal, many vestries and congregations are beginning to run their churches not on the model of democracy, fighting for majority votes and "winning" resolutions. They are ready, on the contrary, to wait upon the Spirit to bring unanimity before proceeding with any policy. Many priests and people from congregations where this is the practice are ready to testify that such a method of running the church is far more streamlined, efficient, and speedy in practice than the old, tired models of democracies and resolutions that seek to organize the church along the lines of governments and secular councils.[24]

There is a word of good news here for the Episcopal Church today. General Convention seems to lurch from one controversial issue to another until the gospel itself seems to be reduced to one issue or another, as though the good news of Jesus Christ were just another ideology. Christianity is not an ideology. Christianity is not any *thing*. Christianity is some *body*—the body of Christ. In the life of that body, if there is to be health and unity, there must be no place for rivalry, competition, or empire building. Of course there is a real place for controversy, serious engagement, and disagreement. But that is not the same thing as monomania, the tyranny of single-issue (church) politics. For no one issue is bigger than the gospel and we must refuse to turn into absolutes

any *thing* over and above the life of the total body whose members
we are in a rich and colorful diversity. The monomaniac becomes
a tyrant to the body (however idealistic his or her issues or concerns may be). That is not the model for the Christian church.
But,

> speaking the truth in love, we are to grow up in every way
> into him who is the head, into Christ, from whom the whole
> body joined and knit together by every joint with which it
> is supplied, when each part is working properly, makes bodily
> growth and upbuilds itself in love.[25]

THE HOLY SPIRIT AND CHURCH GROWTH

Then furthermore, the Holy Spirit quickens the conscience. He
gives us the spirit of discernment whereby we see and hate sin
and we see and love righteousness. For whenever and wherever
the Holy Spirit comes and is at work, he convinces the world of
sin, of righteousness, and of judgment.[26] Wherever the light
shines brightest, there dust and dirt are most clearly in evidence.
"I hate the sins that made thee mourn and drove thee from my
breast."[27] There is no room, however, in the life of the spirit for
moralism. That merely breeds guilt and guilt is little more than
wounded pride. On the contrary, the enlightenment of the Spirit
draws attention primarily to Jesus and only then (as best my soul
can bear) does he show up sin for what it is—alienation from
God, unlovely and unloving. It is only *after* the vision of the
holiness of God in the temple, that Isaiah was aware of his sin:
"Woe is me for I am a man of unclean lips and I dwell amidst a
people of unclean lips."[28] That is repentance, individual and corporate. Furthermore it is the work of the Spirit quickening the
conscience which makes evident and present the beauty and holiness of Christ. And then it is not just a matter of personal piety
but a genuine and corporate summons to confession of sin, both
in the individual, in the church, and in society. Christians must
not be shocked by sin. We are repelled by it but always in the
direction of God.

There is no room for judgmentalism. We are compassionate

toward the sinner, but we hate the sin. Neither is there any room for that moralism which would encourage us to sweep the room clean and leave it empty: cleanliness for its own sake. Our awareness of sin comes as we walk ever more closely with God. That journey and that awareness are always in tandem, leaving no room between our avoidance of sin and our pursuit of holiness for the devil of self-sufficiency or self-righteousness to enter in. And if there is no room for moralism, then there will be no room for triumphalism either. We know we are in need of forgiveness daily—that we are powerless over sin. For when the Holy Spirit is not moving and working in the church, it is not long before we begin to see the marks of complacency and triumphalism. A church that is informed and enthused by the Holy Spirit, however, will be reformed and renewed by repentance at every step and will in its turn do whatever it can to change society and to refashion it more and more in line with the designs of the kingdom of God. "The Lord loves those who hate evil"[29] and a church that is continually refreshed and enlightened by the Holy Spirit will be recalled and will recall others to righteousness and godliness.

Finally, in recounting this work of the Holy Spirit, we find that it is the Holy Spirit who in all these ways listed above forms, re-forms, and renews the church as surely as he did at that first Pentecost. He pushes the church around and locates it for mission out in the desert (or the equivalent of the desert in the life of our world) and in the environment of contemporary society. Of course such renewal is uncomfortable, untidy, and at times deeply disturbing. A renewed church will need ordering, but not for ordering's sake. Good orchestras do not like demonstrative conductors who throw themselves around and draw attention to themselves. A good conductor respects the musicianship of each member of the orchestra and knows that his prime task is to bring coordination and an overall exuberance out of the orchestra. The ordained ministry is there to bring about a similar coordination and a similar exuberance but must at all times respect the discipleship of each member. There is, however, going to be a lot of noise and at times obvious mistakes. For such is the price you pay (which in the church has already been paid, thank God) for individuals coming alive and contributing to the overall life of the larger body. Of course, wherever the church is most refreshed and strengthened by the Holy Spirit, you are never very far away from the devil. A nice church probably will not have many problems from the devil. After all, he is a parasite and he is a strategist. He is not going to waste what little time he has left with nice, complacent churches. But wherever the church is coming alive in the spirit, wherever Jesus is glorified, there you will find the devil (as on the night of the Last Supper) right at your elbow.

Yet in all these ways we can speak of renewal in the church through the working of the Holy Spirit, because first and foremost we are already experiencing it in the church today. Old party lines are being transcended. The church is becoming the church. There is a new convergence of the saints beyond where any of us by our own strengths or our own insights would ever have discerned. In all of this our own godliness is always part of the goal and spirituality is the record of our daily journeyings ever closer to God. In this process, theology has its place, as food and fuel for the journey. There need be nothing mindless in this pursuit, because by God's grace, we know that we have the mind of Christ. And furthermore in our pilgrimage we have a keen sense of anticipation, knowing that what he has begun he will perfect. Already we have a foretaste of that kingdom where God reigns, where Christ is glorified, and where he is all in all, already here in time, and for ever in eternity.

Notes

1. Philippians 3:12ff.
2. John 16:13.
3. Romans 6:1.

4. Luke 2:25ff.
5. Matthew 5:3 (New English Bible).
6. Luke 11:13.
7. John 16:14.
8. John 15:13.
9. John 16:12.
10. John 16:13.
11. John 16:15.
12. Anthony Bloom, *God and Man* (London: Darton, Longman & Todd, 1971), p. 69.
13. John Newton, "How sweet the name of Jesus sounds," *The Hymnal 1982*, No. 644.
14. Romans 13:14.
15. Luke 24:27.
16. Romans 8:26.
17. A. M. Ramsey, *The Gospel and the Catholic Church* (London: Longmans, 1936).
18. Matthew 18:20.
19. See Luke 24:34ff.
20. 1 Corinthians 14:23f.
21. Ephesians 4:13.
22. Ephesians 4:15.
23. See 1 Corinthians 12:14ff.
24. See Chapter Nine, p. 000.
25. Ephesians 4:15ff.
26. John 16:8.
27. William Cowper, "O for a closer walk with God," *The Hymnal 1982*, No. 683.
28. Isaiah 6:5.
29. Psalm 34:16.

FIVE

Renewal and Anglican Responsibility in the Worldwide Church

THE RELIGIOUS SCENE IN AMERICA TODAY

Just try it sometime. At any gathering in the Episcopal church. Ask from those present for those who are cradle Episcopalians to raise their hands. Then ask for those who became Episcopalians later in life also to raise their hands. The latter group are always substantially and significantly in the majority. Does this tell us anything about the Episcopal church and the wider fellowship of Anglican churches throughout the world? In all our discussions about Anglicanism (and there are roughly seventy million Anglicans worldwide) we must remember that the Episcopal Church, with about three million members, is a very small part of the whole worldwide scene. The Church of England from which worldwide Anglicanism is derived is even smaller, rather pathetically so, in fact. It is now down to only 1.2 million at the last count in 1985. The largest parts numerically of Anglicanism worldwide, and in terms of growth, are of course the black Anglican churches of Africa, which are expanding at such a rate that it is scarcely possible to keep the structures and hierarchy of those churches in step with the prodigious growth occurring at grass-roots level.

But back again to the American scene. Any European visiting

America, or coming to live here, cannot but be struck by the place of religion in American life in the closing years of the twentieth century. In America, all the churches have a prominent part in the life of society and something like between fifty and sixty percent of the population are present in the total of the many different churches on Sundays. That has to be a fact of considerable significance. The leading nation in the world is still a religious nation. That is in sharp contrast with the deeply rooted secularism of Europe in general and the United Kingdom in particular. In America people are still (on the whole) going to church.

In the spectrum of religious activity in the United States, there is a fervent and substantial presence of protestant fundamentalist sects, powerfully in evidence in the media and strongly to the right politically. Such sects have a high religious profile; they have set their face courageously and sturdily against any form of secularism. They preach with power and authority from the Scriptures, which are unequivocally and in every way the inspired, inerrant word of God down to the last iota. They are a prosperous industry with apparently no shortage of money for their many and ambitious projects. Furthermore (as was so clearly indicated in the presidential election in 1984), they are a political force with which any astute politician must reckon. It is true that such churches often encourage a mindless enthusiasm, which seems to take over the life of their disciples. Nevertheless, it has to be admitted that in an age of fragmentation, drugs, and relativism in morals and truth, their witness is powerful and their influence is substantial.

Then of course there is the massive and impressive presence of the Roman Catholic church. In spite of the sizable problem of a shortage of priests to serve that Communion, its numbers and their influence continue to grow. Furthermore, the renewal movement in the Roman Catholic Church associated with Vatican II is swiftly and strongly in evidence in the United States. Roman Catholics in America went further and deeper in changes than perhaps any other Roman Catholics elsewhere in the world (with the possible exception of Holland). So deep and so far did they go in fact, that the present Pope could be forgiven for thinking that perhaps renewal has gone far enough in the American part of the Roman church. From a church renowned for its uniformity in belief and its impressive monolithic structure of dogma and hierarchy, suddenly wild pluralism is all too much in evidence. Sadly, however, during the eighties and especially under Pope John Paul, the Roman church has suffered two blows. Suddenly there is a new emphasis upon a kind of fundamentalism in sexual morality (conspicuously of course in the practice of birth control). Second, there is a reaction against some of the wilder and more untidy forms of renewal and a command to return to the clericalism so rife prior to Vatican II. This return to clericalism in the Roman Catholic church is certainly at the expense of the role of the laity and also conspicuously plays down the place of Scripture and the use of the mind and reason in the formation of Christian discipleship.

Where then does this leave the minute Episcopal church in the USA? Numerically the Episcopal church had hemorrhaged over one million members between the fifties and the eighties and at one point could have appeared to be going out of business by the close of the century. Certainly if the downward trend of those years had continued, whatever was left of the Episcopal church in the year 2000 would be so irrelevant as to be little more than an ecclesiastical joke. But in its darkest hour, and at its lowest ebb, God, it would appear, has intervened. Yes—nothing less than such an intervention can be claimed if we are to make sense of the vocation of the Episcopal church and look with some confidence toward the year 2000. A similar situation occurred in the Church of England as long ago as 1832. It was in that year that Thomas Arnold remarked, "The Church of England as it now stands no human power can save." He was right, in more ways than he himself realized. What he had failed to reckon with, of course, was that there is another power beyond human power, and it is this power that is the only power really worth having. For the power of God is always best discovered in the life of mankind when we are at our weakest. It is at precisely the moment of breakdown that God breaks through. And so with hindsight, history does not record the final demise of the Church of England in that year of 1832. On the contrary, it seizes upon that very year as the beginning of the great renewal movements issuing out of Oxford and Cambridge and also as the very moment when the largest missionary expansion in the whole history of the church began. In other words the Episcopal church should take heart at this low point in its membership and realize that in some sense we have been this way before.

RENEWAL AND THE FAILURE OF LIBERALISM

Bishop Alden Hathaway, in his introduction to the Winter Park Conference of renewal leaders of the Episcopal church in 1986, spoke boldly: "We are beginning now to be confident that the numbers (of members of the Episcopal church) have reached the bottom and are beginning to climb up." Furthermore, he added: "Let us make sure that the church understands why. For without the renewal movement, those figures would still be on the way down."

These are significant words and they are true. The Episcopal church needs to hear them clearly. For the liberal experiment of creedal laissez-faire prevalent in the Episcopal church over the last forty years has proved to be in practice a spectacular and massive failure. That also needs to be said loud and clear. It is bankrupt spiritually and economically. It is simply not making any new Christians because it has failed to make Christians new. It tailors and trims the scriptural gospel of Jesus Christ until that gospel has no resources and no power with which to speak to peoples' lives in their needs and crises. "The man who marries the spirit in one age," wrote the craggy Dean Inge of St. Paul's Cathedral, London, "will be a widower in the next." The liberal and modernist movements in the church certainly wed the spirit of the 50s and 60s and now appear somewhat estranged widows in the 1980s. There are still certainly a lot of ecclesiastical widows around, still muttering the slogans and shibboleths of the 50s, but without anyone to hear them. Liberal protestantism, like the deism and theism of the enlightenment in the Church of England

in the eighteenth century, is powerless to win souls for Jesus Christ
in an age that is further over the precipice than it was in the
balmy and confident days of America (and in England for that
matter) immediately after World War II. Those were very different
times. The situation has changed. The situation is more serious
and the issues are more acute.

Liberal protestantism appears to work as we might expect in
a comfortable middle-class society sitting on beanbag chairs and
discussing social problems in an environment of the campus and
in an age of secular confidence. It projects ideas and issues; it is
conspicuous as an ideology with a strong political bias. But place
such disciples in the depressed areas of large industrial cities or
in multi-racial and poor areas and frankly it has no gospel to
proclaim that can be heard and received by the very people that
Christ regarded as the ultimate test for all ministry and evangelism—the poor. It is the very rich and the very poor who receive
the full apostolic gospel of salvation most readily. They are both
at risk and they know it. To say this does not mean that many
issues and concerns of the liberals and the modernists should not
be concerns for the church. What it does say, however, is that
the gospel cannot be emptied out of all its content and be left
with only issues, concerns, and problems. The gospel speaks of
promises rather than problems, of community and celebration before it speaks of groups and discussions.

Little wonder therefore that people in the Episcopal church
have voted in recent years with their feet and also, it must be
said, with their pocketbooks. Several dioceses have been forced
to cut back on diocesan staff through lack of money, which in
turn is the direct result of this lack of membership and frankly
the absence of people in pews on Sundays. Those same dioceses
are often conspicuous for their liberal persuasions. Where there
is renewal, the bills are not a problem. There is always enough
money to pay the bills and to give away afterward for those very
concerns to which liberals wish to draw our attention, and rightly
so: but only if we get first things first. For the point made here is
that liberalism in our church is in fact a parasite; it is producing
no new life. That needs to be said clearly and loudly and the

challenge needs to be put on record. The faithful are continuing to vote and will continue to vote with their feet. So beware!

But it is, as we have said, at such a moment as this that God acts and renewal in our church is most evident, not only because it is making Christians new but because it is also making some new Christians. The numbers have bottomed out and are on the increase. Bishop Alden Hathaway is under no illusions as to the reason for this. "We must claim for renewal the recent turn around in membership and stewardship in the Episcopal church, reversing the downward slide of the last 25 years." The ingredients of that renewal are to be found in a re-affirmation of belief—a full-blooded, apostolic, scriptural, catholic, and thinking Christianity. Nothing less than that must be our goal because nothing less than that can be effective in renewing the church and in its turn in reforming and renewing society. Of course, the temptation to swing from a liberalism dominated by human reason to a fundamentalism devoid of reason is always strong. But that is not the answer. Two wrongs do not make a right even if it is a political right!

THE RESPONSIBILITY OF THE EPISCOPAL CHURCH

It is at this point that we need to re-affirm and re-assert the peculiar and special beliefs and insights of the Episcopal church in particular and of Anglicanism in general. For although Anglicanism is pluralistic (deliberately) in its beliefs and practices, it does have parameters to its creeds, and it is a church that most certainly seeks to speak with authority and precision. It is often derided by its critics as a church of compromise. That allegation is not true. Anglicanism is indeed comprehensive but at its best it is comprehensive for the sake of truth and it does not seek to compromise for the sake of peace. In the turbulent years of the Reformation and Counter-Reformation, when many lost their heads, either literally or metaphorically, Anglicanism, by opting neither for the fundamentalism of the Scriptures in the protestant churches or the security of ecclesiasticism in the Roman church, struck out in a yet more excellent way. The Church of England, from which Anglicanism is derived, set out on a course with real theological foundations, with a proper and powerful doctrine of authority. It witnessed to a robust Christian faith in an age of fragmentation, party strife, and disintegration.

There is an overwhelming need for that same sanity of comprehensiveness in the religious climate of America today. Such is the contribution the Episcopal church can and should be making in our own age. It is in some sense, as it was in the sixteenth and seventeenth centuries, "the mean between two extremes."[1] The extremes are all too evident in the contemporary religious climate of America. We have looked at some of them briefly. They constitute a challenge to the Episcopal church. For it is precisely in this sort of climate that Episcopalians need to recover their roots, extend their branches, and begin again to bear the fruits and life of the spirit. Thank God it is already happening wherever renewal is evident. And that renewal for Episcopalians means a re-affirmation of the gospel with the proper authority with which Anglicanism can and has spoken whenever it has been faithful to its true credentials.

AUTHORITY IN ANGLICANISM

The Anglican church, unlike many of the churches of the Reformation, is not, has never been, and cannot be a confessional church. Because Anglicanism goes right back in unbroken succession to the apostles, it does not have, as churches that began at the Reformation tend to have, a doctrinal statement or confession of its faith. Furthermore, unlike the Roman Catholic church it does not have a hierarchical constitution that promulgates clear or even infallible statements to which scholarly inquiry may have recourse. Rather than pointing to well-manicured statements, Anglicanism points us to a method and process by which we can do our ongoing homework of theology. The Thirty-nine Articles of Religion bound in with the Book of Common Prayer at the Reformation point primarily to Scripture as being the fundamental base of authority for the church and its doctrine. "Show us anything set forth in Holy Scripture," wrote Bishop Stephen Neill in his book on Anglicanism, "that we do not teach, and we will teach it; show us anything in our teaching and practice that is plainly contrary to Holy Scripture, and we will abandon it."[2] Yes, that is our position—officially at least, although some bishops and leaders in Anglicanism today appear to choose to ignore their own credentials. As Richard Hooker, the father of Anglicanism, wrote in the sixteenth century: "What scripture doth plainly deliver, it is to that the first place both of credit and obedience is due."[3] Or in the blunt and direct words of Article VI:

> Holy Scripture containeth all things necessary to salvation:
> so that whatsoever is not read therein, nor may be proved
> thereby, is not to be required of any man, that it should be
> believed as an article of the Faith, or be thought requisite or
> necessary to salvation.

Yet in Anglicanism we come to the witness of Scripture and read it through the spectacles of tradition and reason. Unlike the Reformation churches, it is not a case for Anglicans merely of *sola scriptura*. We come to Scriptures with a perspective of the traditions and teachings of the church, its worship and its creeds, its sacraments and its threefold ordained ministry of deacon, priest, and bishop. Here is the environment of faith in which the word of Scripture is preached, received, and obeyed. Our church is truly scriptural in shape and in its turn it prays and validates Scripture in its corporate life. The word of God and the people of God witness to each other.

Furthermore, as Anglicans we come to Scripture with our minds and with our experience of the Spirit of God uniting with our human spirit. Sometimes this is baldly called "reason." But reason, on the lips of sixteenth- and seventeenth-century divines before the "age of reason," was a much fuller word than it is for us today. It meant so much more than mere cerebral processes. It really involved the whole of our human insight. And it is that, and nothing less than that, that Anglicans believe should be brought to bear along with tradition upon our reading of the Scriptures. But beware! Explicitly, casuistry, and rational games are not permitted. Medieval philosophy in the guise of casuistry

could twist any text to mean anything it wanted it to mean.
Hence the preamble to the Thirty-nine Articles, specifically
warns us:

> No man hereafter shall either print, or preach to draw the
> article aside any way, but shall submit to it in the plain and
> full meaning thereof: and shall not put his own sense or
> comment to be the meaning of the article, but shall take it
> in the literal and grammatical sense.[4]

In other words what the creeds say and state they mean. There
is no place in Anglicanism for abuse of reason that permits black
to be called white or vice versa.

So if we are faithful to our Anglican credentials, we shall be
recalled continually in our day to a new sense of obedience as a
church. We shall be aware that we are a church and a people
under authority. We shall receive with gratitude God's definitive
revelation of himself in Jesus Christ, the Word made flesh, and
we shall discern that word primarily through the words of Scripture, enlightened by the traditions and experience of the church
over two thousand years. That revelation and that word will be
informed by human reason, experience, and the evidence of the
created world around us and within us. In other words, authority
is dynamic for Anglicanism and not static. It is a process and not
a product. So Archbishop Michael Ramsey wrote:

> While the Anglican church is vindicated by its place in his-
> tory with a strikingly balanced witness to gospel and church
> and sound learning, its greater vindication lies in its pointing
> through its own history to something of which it is a frag-
> ment. Its credentials are its incompleteness, with the tension
> and the travail in its soul. It is clumsy and untidy, it baffles
> neatness and logic. For it is sent not to commend itself "as
> the best type of Christianity" but by its very brokeness to
> point to the universal Christ wherein all have died.[5]

So let us be quite clear: the Episcopalian is called to live in
obedience under the revelation of God (untidy at the edges though
it may be) and as a disciple under authority. In an age and culture
that reveres (some would even say idolizes) individual freedom

and autonomy, the Episcopalian rejoices to affirm that the church is under the authority of God, the Father, revealed in the Son, and apprehended by the Holy Spirit at work in the heart, mind, and life of the faithful disciple. Christ is Lord of the church and Lord of the Scriptures, and neither the Bible nor the church can be worshipped. Neither can usurp the unique lordship of Christ— God's definitive and last word to us.

Yes, of course such a system is untidy. Anglicanism has always frankly acknowledged that there will be disagreement at the edges, and therefore, it has deliberately refrained from multiplying those kinds of doctrines which are defined as "necessary to salvation." Such doctrines in Anglicanism are (praise God) kept to a minimum. This process of restraint was spoken of by Anglicans in the nineteenth century as "a reserve in the communicating of Christian knowledge." The gospel endorses this kind of restraint without which discipleship is reduced to legalism and creates burdens too heavy to bear—burdens that neither us nor our fathers could bear. Yet, at the same time, it does not permit reason or any part of the tripartite system to play tyrant in this precious and important process—that tripartite of Scripture, Sacraments and the human spirit. For Scripture teaches us that while we must love the Lord with our minds, those minds left to themselves without the influence of the Holy Spirit and constant renewal, will soon become squeezed back into the mold of the prejudices and blindnesses that are characteristic of the secular life of the age in which we live. For we most certainly do *not* live in an age that is open-minded. We live in a time when culture conditions our thinking and our outlook in wildly prejudiced ways. The Christian needs his mind continually reconditioned by the culture and outlook of the Scriptures, so that he can say with St. Paul, "We have the mind of Christ."[6] Such reasoning will need to be fashioned by the school of Scripture and the traditions and experience of the church. Reason, for a Christian, is faithful and reliable in so far as it accords primarily with the record of Scripture, and secondarily as it draws on the evidence of truth latent in the texture of God's world, observable through the sciences and apprehended both by our mind and our senses. Reason is thus a valuable but fallible guide that must be submitted at all times to a scriptural way of seeing God's world. Reason, defined and formed by the authority of Scripture and illumined by the Holy Spirit, is certainly a potentially very strong ally and a reliable guide for the church. We do not need to flee to a mindless Christianity in order to rescue our faith from compromise and anarchy.

In all this discussion, renewal is recalling us to a way of reading the Scriptures, exercising our reason, and using our traditions under the Lordship of Christ. There is no doubt that all three evidences of God's word have at some point played tyrant in this process of distilling authority and revelation in Anglicanism.

> Neither the Scriptures, nor the traditions of the church (and we could also add reason) can be given that ultimate and unquestioned authority that belongs to God alone. Biblical and ecclesiastical fundamentalisms are as idolatrous as they are irrational. If the special temptation of the liberal tradition is to echo without criticism the voice of the present age, the special temptation of both the catholic and evangelical traditions is to echo without criticism the voices of previous ages. The work of discerning the doctrine that sets forth a life in Christ demands from Christian disciples all the powers of insight of that intellect and conscience which they can bring to the task. Because God graciously respects the humanity of those to whom he gives himself, while at the same time remaining infinitely beyond their grasp, there is bound to be a many-sidedness to the apprehension and expression of the gospel. The need for comprehensiveness in the church derives, therefore, from a proper recognition of the complementarities of the Christian response to the gospel, not from easy going accommodation and compromise.[7]

AUTHORITY AND OBEDIENCE

In the last word, God's revelation speaks to us with authority and demands a response. That response is summarized in one word: obedience. If authority is a hard word for the twentieth century, obedience is no less easy for us to swallow. Yet there comes a point in renewal when the proper response is no longer further discussions, sub-committees, or even writing another book. The proper response to God's revelation is to go out and act upon it in faith and obedience. That is the only way we find that it works. That is the witness of all the renewal movements at the present time. Wherever we strike out in obedience, the proof of the theological pudding is always discovered in the evangelistic eating. God's word is powerful and never returns to him empty-handed. It fulfills that for which it was sent out. The measure of Christ's authority in the New Testament and especially in the fourth gospel, is in exact proportion to his loving obedience to his Father. It took a centurion (a man working within authority structures) to spot authority when he saw it. "I say to one 'Go' and he goes and to another, 'Come' and he comes."[8] There are two words in Latin for authority: *auctoritas* and *imperium.* Jesus rejects the latter—all imperialistic authority—in front of Pilate. Nevertheless, Jesus is a man of authority—*auctoritas*—because he is first a man of obedience. The Father sent him: "Go and he goes." The mission of the church is the mission of the Father's word. "My word!" he says. And we need to take him at his word.

Renewal in all the churches today is found wherever Christians are taking God at his word. In spite of all the untidy edges to many Christian discussions today, there is enough mainstream evidence of God's word in Scripture, discerned through reason, and tested in the life and worship of the church, to move disciples from the paralysis of analysis to becoming apostolic agents of the gospel and the revelation of God's loving purposes through Jesus Christ in the world. The Scriptures are the record of that revelation. The church is a witness to the authority and authenticity of that revelation. And the resurrection of Jesus Christ in his body the church is the proof that this revelation is true and effective.

A church conditioned and fashioned and energized by that revelation will be powerful when it speaks to our world, to America, and to this age. It will be a scriptural, catholic, thinking church with a genius to avoid the extremes that are so evident in the spectrum of religion in America. It could be that it is for this very hour that Anglicanism has been so wonderfully empowered by God through the ages. It could be that it is no accident that in any Episcopal gathering, as we saw at the beginning of this chapter, there is always a majority of those who have chosen Anglicanism in adult life over those who were simply cradle Episcopalians. Certainly there is already ample evidence, for example, among evangelicals who today have found the Anglican way a richer church and a fuller gospel.[9] Many other church people (conspicuously and sadly even Roman Catholics) are looking to Anglicanism as a church for a thinking, catholic, and scriptural laity. In many ways Anglicanism is emerging as a prototype of the new world ecumenism—that one church for which Christ prays. If those words seem too heady and too ambitious perhaps we need to hear that very testimony from the pen of a Roman Catholic Benedictine scholar:

> All Anglican Churches, however, are one in their conscious endeavor to preserve the Apostolic faith and character of the church's worship of the first centuries, though trying to incorporate in it the contributions of the Reformation and those of their own time so far as they have positive and permanent value. This typical Anglican attitude in respect of tradition and enrichment is at the basis of the moderation and comprehensiveness of Anglicanism. It marks world-Anglicanism as being, as it were, a provisional prototype of the re-united *Ecumene,* the world Christianity of the future. That Anglicanism comprises only a small number of Christians does not detract from that fact.[10]

The times are urgent and the days are evil. The responsibility for Anglicanism in general and for the Episcopal church in particular is overwhelming in its implications precisely because God requires much from those to whom much has been given.

Notes

1. Preface to the *Book of Common Prayer*, Church of England, 1662.
2. Stephen Neill, *Anglicanism* (Harmondsworth: Penguin, 1958), p. 418.
3. Richard Hooker, *Laws of Ecclesiastical Polity*, Book V, chapter 8, section 11.
4. Preamble to Thirty-nine Articles, *Book of Common Prayer*, 1662.
5. A. M. Ramsey, *The Gospel and the Catholic Church* (London: Longmans, 1936).
6. 1 Corinthians 2:16.
7. Peter Baelz, "Reconsidering Anglicanism's Interdependent Traditions," *The Times*, 27 November 1982.
8. Matthew 8:9.
9. See Robert Webber, *Evangelicals on the Canterbury Trail* (Waco, Texas: Word, 1985).
10. W. H. Van De Pol, *Anglicanism in Ecumenical Perspective* (Pittsburgh: Duquesne University Press, 1965), p. 34.

SIX

Renewal and the Word of God

FUNDAMENTALISM?

We must grasp the nettle! The nettle is of course the authority of Scripture. It is not sufficient to define belief by what we do *not* believe. It is no earthly use for the Episcopal church to continue to say that we are not fundamentalists. If we are not fundamentalists in our convictions about Scripture, then what are we? If we do not believe that the fundamentalist sects are right in the way in which they use and believe the Scriptures, then it is not unfair to ask the question: "Well, what is the right way to use the Scriptures, and in what sense can we believe the Bible to be the word of God?"

For there is a crisis for our church in this area and we simply have to face up to it. Seminarians, on the whole, leave seminary today with just sufficient knowledge of the history of scriptural criticism from the German Tübingen school of the mid-nineteenth century, through to Buber and Bultmann of the twentieth century, to have lost their nerve on the authority of Scripture. The central board of the platform for their preaching and apol-

For much of the content of this chapter the author is indebted to the Rev. Peter C. Moore, who lectured at the Winter Park Conference.

ogetics has been pulled from under them, and this shows all too
clearly to a laity hungry for the word of God. We have to admit
that the substantial drift to the fundamentalist churches with
their emphasis upon and love for the Scriptures is a judgment
upon the mainstream churches in America. If, in order to love
the Scriptures and to find their power at work in Christian discipleship, it is necessary to seek out the fundamentalist churches,
then that is a judgment upon us. If the fundamentalist churches
are the places where you hear the word of God preached with
conviction and with power, then what do you hear preached in
the mainstream churches?

At the Reformation, the Anglican church affirmed the place
and power of Scripture in the life of the church. The Episcopal
church today should be conspicuous as a scriptural church. Furthermore, at the Reformation it was Dean Colet of St. Paul's,
London, who himself was conspicuous in the revitalization of
scriptural preaching. It is in *our* mandate. It is in our very blood-
stream. After all there is probably more Scripture per square foot
in the liturgy of the Episcopal church than in the liturgy of any
of the other churches. Since the Reformation, clergy and laity
alike have been encouraged to read Morning and Evening Prayer,
which are essentially Bible-centered daily offices, and which give
substantial passages of Scripture for our daily bread and for our
daily discipleship. Whatever other adjective you may wish to add
to the noun of the Episcopal church in particular or Anglicanism
at large, the first and last qualifying adjective must be scriptural.
Bishop Stephen Neill in his book on Anglicanism, speaks eloquently of

> the biblical quality by which the whole warp and woof of
> Anglican life is penetrated. At every point the theological
> appeal is to Scripture. Article eight of the thirty-nine arti-
> cles tells us that the creeds are accepted and recited because
> they may be proved by "most certain warrants of holy scrip-
> ture." The Anglican churches read more of the bible to the
> faithful than any other group of churches.[1]

So what has happened to us all? In practice throughout the

whole of this century the encroachment of modernism in biblical scholarship and the way that scholarship has been prescribed to seminarians and laity alike make those words of Stephen Neill ring hollow, empty, and false. Professor R. H. Lightfoot (a relatively conservative scholar) concluded a lifetime of biblical scholarship as a renowned Anglican with an observation that would appear to leave little in the Scriptures and even in the Gospels that we can rely upon in any sense as gospel truth:

> The form of the earthly no less than of the heavenly Christ is for the most part hidden from us. For all the inestimable value of the Gospels, they yield little more than a whisper of his voice; we trace in them but the outskirts of his ways. [2]

Is that really so?

EXPERIENCING THE SCRIPTURES

We have to say quite frankly that such an assessment is not the experience of renewed Christians in renewed parts of the church today, and surely it is from that end of the problem that we should begin our discussions. We should begin where all good theology begins: how can we make sense of what we have experienced? The question that biblical theology and biblical scholarship alike has to address must surely be this: how can we begin to explain the power of the Scriptures in the experience and life of the church? What is the quality and source of the power of Scripture in the experience of the church over two thousand years as well as in our own experience? For the work of all theology (as with all sciences) is to seek an explanation of something we have already discovered as truth. It should not start the other way round and seek to deny the discovery because it does not fit into the prejudices and assumptions of the formulas of science. The discovery will demand a re-writing of those formulas, if necessary. And yet Professor Nineham is doing the very opposite of this in his narrow-minded and prejudiced statement, when he writes:

> Since the historians' essential criteria presuppose the absence of abnormality or discontinuity, only those events can

be described as "historical" which are fully and exclusively
human and entirely confined within the limits of this world.[3]

If such is the case, perhaps it is time for the historians to question
some of their presuppositions and pursue their discipline with a
more scientific approach to their craft. In other words, it is time
for them to narrate and explain what the evidence of millions of
men and women have discovered as historically true. After all, it
is only a question of deciding whose prejudices will be accepted
as the premise for all else that follows!

The "prejudices" of renewal presuppose that when the word
of God is read by the people of God in the environment of the
Spirit of God, we experience and discover the presence of God
speaking to us. The word he speaks, in a word, is Jesus. For in
spite of all the problems of historicity and many questions that
we will rightly wish to continue asking about the Bible, the basic
discovery is that there is a unique power in the words of the
Scriptures. The task and problem of theology is to seek some kind
of explanation that will refuse to talk in terms of magic on the
one hand or to claim clearly disprovable credentials of inerrancy
on the other hand. So let us begin with the experience of the
church.

Like it or not, this book keeps its word and its promises.
Something happens when we read it. It has the power to make
Jesus (the word of God) present to us. It forms and conforms the
life of the church and the Christian to that living word, discerned
through the spoken, written, and printed word. That is what
happened to St. Augustine in the garden on a hot summer's after-
noon as long ago as 386 A.D. That is what happened to Antony
of Egypt when he heard and received the gospel being read in the
liturgy of the day. It changed his life. Jesus spoke directly to him.
That is what happened when Pascal on that strange and beautiful
night was reading the seventeenth chapter of St. John's gospel.
There were tongues of fire and the presence of Jesus was devas-
tatingly evident to him. So real was that experience to this deeply
thinking and intellectual man that he wrote down the record of
that experience and pinned it in the lining of his jacket over his

heart for the rest of his life. That is what happened when Archbishop Anthony Bloom read at one sitting St. Mark's gospel. Jesus
was made present in the room with him.

And so we could go on and on recounting the experiences of
the church and our own experiences of the word of God in Scripture. The task of theology is to seek to make some sort of sense
of these experiences and not to tell us that we should not have
those experiences because theologians have decided that the
Scriptures are not that kind of book. We must not be told by
theologians that we cannot have these experiences because their
presuppositions on certain issues about Scripture deny that the
Scriptures are different in any particular way from any other book.
Of course all that the theologians will tell us about the dating,
and the manner in which the Scriptures were written, is of interest and important in our study of the Scriptures. Nevertheless
it has to be admitted that it is largely of academic interest and
not frankly of prime importance either for the preacher or for the
disciple. For all our theology is necessarily subsequent to the event
of reading and receiving the word of God in Scripture.

That is the only way we can tackle sacramental theology. We
should not say that the bread is not body because you cannot find
an adequate philosophical formula to explain the reality which
the church experiences. God's people when they partake of the
bread and drink the cup over two thousand years have experienced
the unique presence and power of Jesus Christ at work in their
lives. Of course you must test the claims of eucharistic experience
and that is also part of the task of theology. You must rescue
theology from magic. But you must go beyond that and seek then
to formulate some adequate explanation of the insistent testimony
of the church that Jesus Christ, the Lord, is present.

THEOLOGY AND THE WORD OF GOD

That surely is the way we must tackle all theology of the biblical
experience of the church over the past two thousand years, seeking as best we can some kind of theological formulas of explanation. (Knowing as we do in sacramental theology that all

formulas will be inadequate and in some sense unsatisfying.) For in practice it is always true that

> the clarity of an explanation seems to depend upon the de-gree of satisfaction that it affords . . . "explanation" may perhaps be roughly defined as a restatement of something in terms of current interests and assumptions . . . all depends upon our presuppositions, which in turn depends upon our training, whereby we have come to regard (or to feel) one set of terms as ultimate, the other not.[4]

So today, we need to recover in the life of the church, in our training of the laity and of ordinands, a way of seeing the Scrip-tures and a right way of reading them, receiving them, marking them, learning them, and inwardly digesting them. We shall lit-erally have to start all over again and learn to read the Bible in the way Christians have read the Scriptures and experienced them over the history of the church. We shall need to use the process of exegesis and seek to discover what the Scriptures meant when they were written and so learn by the indwelling of the Spirit how to move from what they meant to what they mean for us now. In other words, a proper discipline of interpretation. All the other problems of date, authorship, and compilation can and will have their place, more for some than for others. We need not be afraid of that process, because we shall have discerned and made our own that primary and underlying process, namely receiving the word of God as food for the people of God under the direction and guidance of the Holy Spirit of God. We shall then discover the real presence of Jesus as the word of God. We shall discover that this book is indeed a book of presence, power, and authority. For it is not enough to speak simply of the Bible as the record of revelation: it is also that continuing revelation itself, effecting with power what it symbolizes in the words of that revelation. The Word of God again and again makes himself known through the words of Scripture. In one sense it is a charismatic book: something is given and something happens when we read this book. Paul Tournier writes:

> Through the Bible, the book of the word revealed and in-

carnate, . . . God speaks, and personal contact with him is
established. And when it is established, Bible reading is no
longer an irksome effort . . . it becomes a personal dialogue
in which the least word touches us personally.[5]

From another very different tradition, Thomas Merton in his
powerful spiritual autobiography witnessed to the impact of the
Scriptures when he first began to read the Bible.

There was something deep and disturbing in the lines. I
thought they only moved me as poetry; and yet I also felt
. . . that there was something personal about them. God
often talks to us directly in Scripture. . . . He plants the
words full of actual graces as we read them and sudden un-
discovered meanings are sown in our hearts, if we attend to
them, reading with minds that are at prayer. I did not yet
have the art of reading that way, but nevertheless these words
had a dark fire in them with which I began to feel myself
burned and seared.[6]

So in spite of all the problems that such a doctrine of Scripture may present to theologians, we are compelled to speak of the
Bible as the Word of God. It does not mean that we cannot see
the words of Scripture as truly human but in a similar way to the
paradox of the incarnation, we have at the same time to say that
they are also truly the Word of God.

In fact, like the theological battles of the first five centuries
over christological issues, any problems aroused by the experience
of the church are presumably problems for the theologian. The
church was compelled by its experience through prayer and worship to affirm both the humanity and the divinity of Jesus. That
was their underlying experience. Now over to the theologians! Let
us see if they can manufacture a formula and a doctrine that does
justice to these experiences. They had a go, but frankly did not
do a particularly intellectually satisfying job. So with the apparent
contradiction in our theological interpretation of Scripture. The
words are clearly very human words. We are presented at one level
with a very human collection of poetry, history, law, prophecy,
wisdom, biography, apocalyptic, and epistle—all written by hu-

man authors with varying degrees of literary ability. They all used
the thought forms of their day. What else had they to use? Yes,
it is certainly a very human record.

But, writes Peter Moore:

> At the same time we feel compelled to say that it is more
> than just a human book. It is not only a record of revelation,
> it is part of that revelation itself. Without denying that it is
> the words of men, we are certain it is also the Word of God.
> By this we do not mean that the words of men were somehow
> lifted up into the divine purpose, nor do we mean that they
> were divinely dictated, never composed by real human
> beings. On the analogy of Christ, we want to say that the
> Bible is both fully human and fully divine. [7]

Now over to you theologians—try that for size! By all means come
to the words of men and apply criticism and criteria that might
be appropriate in tackling such literature. But for God's sake
(literally) do not stop there. It will be like going to a restaurant
and simply reviewing the menu. Taste and see: you will discover
that this is food indeed, daily bread, the Word of God for the
people of God in the environment of the Spirit of God. Do that
and it will not be long before you will soon be recommending
friends to go to the same restaurant and do likewise!

THE WORD OF GOD AND THE RENEWAL
OF THE PEOPLE OF GOD

The Bible in the experience of the church is indeed the Word of
God. In the first place that is the Bible's own view of itself. Paul
writes, "All Scripture is inspired by God (literally God breathed-
out) and profitable for teaching, for reproof, for correction and
for training in righteousness." [8] Furthermore, the writers in the
New Testament especially claim that what they were writing was
the "living and abiding word of God." [9] Paul states that his writ-
ings are "the Word of God" [10] given in words "not taught by
human wisdom but taught by the Spirit." [11]

But there is a further and perhaps much more important point

that we need to assert as we reclaim the Scriptures as the word
of God. For the truth is that Jesus himself believed the Bible to
be God's authoritative word. He treated it as God's word: "Till
heaven and earth pass away not an iota, not a dot will pass from
the law until it is accomplished."[12] "Scripture cannot be broken."[13]
Furthermore, Jesus—the Word of God—memorizes and interior-
izes and uses the word of God in order to rebuke Satan in the
wilderness in his temptations. In his testimony from the cross and
indeed in discovering his own identity He continues to use and
memorize Scripture. His understanding that Messiah must suffer
was derived from the witness of the Old Testament. In fact we
have a situation in which there is literally a three-fold witness to
the reality of the Bible as the Word of God. It is the Bible's own
view of itself. It is the view of the Scriptures which Jesus held in
his earthly ministry. Finally, it is the view of historic Christianity,
not only in the earliest days of Clement of Rome and Ignatius of
Antioch through to Chrysostom, Origen, Jerome, Augustine, and
many others. Christianity is no longer recognizable as Christianity if it no longer recognizes the Bible as the Word of God.

　　Of course, we can make the mistake of idolizing the Bible—
biliolatry. There is always the temptation to make means an end
in themselves. It is all too easy to make

> the Bible an end in itself, rather than a means to worship,
> obedience, and a growing knowledge of God. When a new
> convert becomes fascinated with Biblical numerology or Bib-
> lical prophecy, or becomes overly eager to prove the scientific
> or historic accuracy of this or that portion of the Bible, then
> they are doing just what Jesus is recorded as cautioning us
> not to do: "You search the Scriptures, because you think
> that in them you have eternal life; and it is they that bear
> witness to me; yet you refuse to come to me that you may
> have life."[14]

For the life is not in them, but through them. The Bible is an
icon; we must learn to see through it and beyond it; otherwise it
will become an idol, an end in itself. Frederick Buechner writes:
"If you look *at* a window, you see fly-specks, dust, the crack where

Juniors' Frisbie hit it. If you look *through* a window, you see the
world beyond."[15] It was Philip Brooks who used to caution us
against such idolatry. The Bible, he said, was like a telescope. If
a man looks through his telescope, he sees worlds beyond; but if
he looks at his telescope he does not see anything but that. The
Bible is a thing to be looked through, to see that which is beyond;
but most people only look at it, and so they see only the dead-
letter.

Presumably that was what Thomas Merton meant when he
spoke of reading the Scriptures "with minds that are at prayer."
There is a new urgency in our church to recover such a proper
way of reading the Scriptures. It needs to be taught in seminaries.
All of God's people need to rediscover a way of reading the Scriptures that belongs to our tradition. We need to read the Scriptures
again in the way that St. Augustine and St. Jerome read the
Scriptures. For in many ways the Scriptures are to the Christian
what the law was to the people of the old Israel. We need to love
the Scriptures in the way that the devout Jew, as seen in
Psalm 119, loved the law of the Lord. He bound it between his
eyes on his forehead and he put it on the doorpost of his house.
We need to receive that word and to interiorize it. We need to
eat it like food, or rather in the same way that a cow eats and
then chews her cud. We need to be fed with the Word of God
in such measure and in such depth that in times of crisis the cud
of these words can be recalled and chewed. So Mary the mother
of the Lord is reported to have meditated upon the mighty acts
of God and to have "kept all these things pondering them in her
heart."[16] So with her son Jesus: at the crisis of Calvary, the words
from the Cross are derived from the Scriptures—a lifetime of
reading, marking, learning, and inwardly digesting. Now in his
pain and agony and from the subconscious memory these "comfortable words" are released into the consciousness or semi-con-
sciousness of his mind.

In a word the church needs to learn again how to read the
Scriptures so that we may receive them for what they are—the
Word of God. We must read with the mind but we must read
with the heart also. Like Augustine we must learn to chew upon

the Word of God and break open the outer meaning to discern
the inner kernel and spiritual meaning of the words. We need to
go back to Bible school and start all over again, beginning with
the seminaries and the clergy who are called primarily to be ministers of God's word. For the sad truth is this: the people are
looking up and are no longer being fed, or as one cynic put it:
the people are fed up and are no longer looking.

READING AND RECEIVING GOD'S WORD:
BIBLE STUDY AND BIBLICAL SCHOLARSHIP

When we learn to read the Word of God under the Spirit of God
as the people of God, "our hearts burn within us"[17] on the road
of our discipleship. All the things in Scripture that relate to the
word of God made flesh (Jesus) become evident and present. The
Holy Spirit takes the words and makes the Word present. Bells
begin to ring; there is a rapport; it is as though the words are in
italics and leap out of the printed pages to speak to us with a new
vitality and a new urgency. There is a resonance as when a note
is struck in a room where there is an open piano with the sus-
taining pedal on. Suddenly the piano string starts to vibrate in
sympathy with the note sounded either in song, whistling, or just
struck. The piano "comes alive" without any notes in the key-
board being pressed. That is the relationship, by analogy, between
the record of revelation and the revelation—each resonates in
sympathy with the other. The story of the people of God, the
record of the mighty acts of God, the story of Jesus, and my story
(in my discipleship) all have a similar shape (all have a similar
frequency). Strike one note and the others come alive in sym-
pathetic response.

Karl Barth, the great Protestant theologian, tells us that the
Bible is like looking out of the window and seeing everybody on
the street shading their eyes with their hands and staring toward
the sky, presumably observing some totally fascinating event. We
can observe them observing. However, what they are observing
is hidden from our view by the ceiling of the room in which we
are located. They are pointing up: they are caught up. They are

speaking strange words which do not make total sense to us. Clearly they are very excited. Something is happening which we are not able to see for ourselves unless and until we break through the window and get where the action is. Something beyond the limits, parameters, and framework of our limited perceptions has caught them up and is seeking to lead them on "from land to land for strange, intense, uncertain, and yet mysteriously well planned service."[18]

What has caught their attention? They are caught up by nothing less than the mighty acts of God himself of which the Bible is the record. Those mighty acts furthermore are acts of absurd contradiction. They are divine jokes, if you like. And the biggest contradiction of all, the mightiest act of God's many mighty acts and the best joke of all (because it is the last laugh) is that ultimate mighty act of contradiction. It is Jesus and the resurrection. When the reader is reflecting upon the record of Scripture something has to happen to the reader (or the congregation listening to the Scriptures being read). It is only when this happens that our world view. begins to make sense and to come alive. We have to get out through that window of which Barth speaks. We have to break through the limitations and cultural barriers of our purely secularized presuppositions and the limitations of our twentieth-century cultural condition. Our little domestic life needs to be turned upside down and to be so displaced and re-located that it brings us right alongside Abraham and Sarah, Isaac, and Jacob, and all God's holy people outside and through that window in the fuller and richer environment of the kingdom.

Now this is a very disturbing process. Nevertheless it is the only way by which we can be re-located where the action is and take our part and place in the continuing drama of which the Scriptures are the record. That is what happened to Mary in St. Luke's account of the Annunciation. She was "greatly troubled" and disturbed by the message of the angel. She did not know whether she was coming or going or in what direction. But, if we learn how to read St. Luke in the way that he intends us to read what he has written, we shall soon see that Mary discovers her identity through the very tradition of which she is a part. If

we will go on and break through the limitations and prejudices
of our twentieth-century world, we also can discover our identity
along with the identity of God's people throughout the ages. For
you discover your identity when you recognize those with whom
you identify. So with Mary. She is a virgin and now she is told
that she is with child. We do not need to hear this message of
the angel and then immediately turn to Isaiah and exercise some
isolated exegesis of the word virgin (which can also mean, just a
young maiden) in Isaiah's prophecy: "A virgin shall conceive."[19]
Mary is a virgin and with child because she is invited by an angel
(possibly, who knows? the very same angel who spoke to Sarah)
to recall that whole tradition of absurd contradiction that goes
back to when it all began. It began of course with Sarah. But
then it always begins with some absurd contradiction. This is
when the good news always begins. It begins now as it began
then with Sarah. Sarah was barren and past the age. Abraham
was certainly past it and left only with the fantasies of an old
man who would speak of children and grandchildren as numerous
as the grains of "sand upon the seashore." In the reality of the
kingdom of this world he could not even manage to have one
child with Sarah!

And then the angel of disturbance comes to them to tell them
that Sarah (you mean, our old Sarah standing over there?) will
be with child next springtime.[20] Well that certainly plays havoc
with any common sense world view. Her response is a very religious one, such a religious one in fact that she does not have an
appropriate and a sensible sense with which to express it. She
degenerates into a fit of the giggles. (She could have wept of
course or spoken in tongues, or looked as though she were drunk
or a thousand and one other of many religious variations on the
limited theme of our human five senses.) So, dear God, you must
be joking! Sarah with child? Yes, of course God is joking. And
the result is the biggest joke of all: Sarah gives birth to a child,
and that child is called appropriately Isaac, which means in He-
brew, a joke.

Now, Mary, can you see the joke? For faith is a bit like a joke,
and if you do not see it, it probably means that you will not get

it. So let's move on a bit. Because this is not the end of the story.
St. Luke wants you to cast your mind back into your tradition
and identify what is happening to you. It has happened before in
the tradition. We have been this way many times before. For
example, there was Hannah.[21] Now she was barren. She was without child. She goes into the temple of God and prays. She really
prays. She prays with that quality and intensity of prayer which
constitutes another religious experience. Her lips are moving, but
there are no words, for she is praying with her heart, indeed she
is praying with her bowels. (Such is the intensity of that prayer
that it upsets the clergy and she is mistaken for some woman who
is drunk. In the light of Pentecost and Sarah's giggles, that might
tell us quite a lot that we need to know about religious experience.
For we sorely need to break out of the mold and prejudices and
limitations of the twentieth-century way of seeing things.) And,
sure enough, Hannah is with child. She sings a little song.[22] It
is a song of contradiction. It is all about turning our world upside
down—about rich people being made poor and poor people being
made rich; about hungry people being fed and about fat people
who are really starving.

Yet Luke in his account of the Annunciation to Mary wants
us to see that Mary in spite of her initial difficulties has really
seen the joke after all. Now she begins to sing a fuller orchestra-
tion of Hannah's song of contradiction. It is called the Magnifi-
cat.[23] To be exact (logical, correct, and all those other utterly
boring and irrelevant things, which are a purely cerebral way of
seeing this gorgeous saga) Luke does not actually say that she sang
it. But you can bet a dollar to a dime she did. For ever since the
event, the church and all those other absurd characters of contradiction over the past two thousand years have spent an awful
lot of time in singing it. It has become *the* song of the church—
the greatest song of contradiction of all contradictions. In fact it
has been set to more settings than most of us have had good
dinners. It celebrates the best joke of all!

So now, Mary, do you begin to see what this is all adding up
to and where it is all leading? In case you are still at a loss to
explain all this, there is Elizabeth your cousin. So if you need

one more clue, Mary, you may need to know that she is barren
and she also is with child! The kingdom is breaking in! Babies
are coming out of the woodwork; these are absurd signs of contradiction and you Mary are the last and the first—the most
absurd—the ultimate contradiction. The virgin of Israel is with
child.

All the record of the Old Testament leads to this point. The
poor have been made rich. The weakest are by God's gift the
most powerful. Saul, the first king of the Jews, is chosen from
the smallest and the least of the tribes of Israel.[24] The good news
is discovered all among the bad news. All time has led to this
ultimate contradiction: we call him Jesus and his resurrection. Of
course it is difficult to get your bearings in the brave new world
of the kingdom. Your senses are insufficient for the task. You need
to learn to look and to listen all over again. There is always an
angel (thank God) at those difficult turning points on the road,
shouting out a few instructions to help you to get your bearings:
"Why go on looking for the living among the dead? He is not
here."[25] They help to keep you on the right road and to keep you
out of the ditch if you will listen to them.

But (and here is the point of this absurd kind of Bible study)
if you are going to see this properly, it is no use reading the Bible
as if it were just any other book. "The trouble is it's not like any
other book," says Frederick Buechner. "To read the Bible as literature is like reading *Moby-Dick* as a whaling manual or the
Brothers Karamazov for its punctuation."[26] Something has to happen to the reader if he is going to get the joke or see the point of
St. Luke's gospel chapter one. We have to discover our identity
by identifying with Mary and through Mary with Abraham and
Sarah, and Isaac, and Hannah, and Elizabeth. We have to get
up from our armchair of observation at a safe distance. Or (to
use Barth's analogy) we need to break through the window between us and the road outside. We need to break out of the
claustrophobic and limited conceptions of the lecture room and
get through that window ("let the reader understand"[27]) and get
out there, as Barth suggests, where all the action is. Because that's
the way it has to be. After all, Mary and Abraham and the others

are not going to leave the life and witness of their experience out there and be squeezed back into our framework, the tyranny of thought and the claustrophobic atmosphere of the twentieth century where we are today. That's such a small world! So if you cannot beat them join them! That is precisely what has to happen to the reader of Scripture.

The Word convenes and constitutes the church. The Word dislocates and re-orientates the church. The church makes the evidence of the word contemporary and existential. And all this (as for Mary at the Annunciation and as for the apostolic band on the mount of the Transfiguration) is the direct result of the overshadowing and the work of the Holy Spirit. After all that (but only after, and not before or instead of) you can read Biblical criticism as long as you like. Of course there are still loose ends and problems and questions to which we do not have easy answers. But such as they are, they arise out of that basic experience which will never permit us to revert to that saddest of all positions, just trying to read the Bible like any other book. For we cannot but "witness to what we have seen and heard."[28] We shall in this way experience the power, authority, and presence of Christ, the word made flesh, uniquely revealed to us in the words of Scripture. Our hearts are on fire with Pentecost and no number of analytical theologians from the fire department can ever put that fire out.

THE WORD OF GOD IN TODAY'S CULTURE

This kind of Bible reading and Bible study infects and affects all our preaching and all the church's teachings that are based upon the Scriptures. It will call the tune, which theologians can then authenticate, in many and varying ways, because we know we have a song to sing, a story to tell and a life to live. Biblical scholarship will not be repressed or ignored, but it will be given its proper place under the baton of the Holy Spirit. Such study and reading of the Scriptures by due recourse to their narrative content and their traditional thought forms will re-shape the content and vocabulary of our counselling and our care for those in need. At least alongside some of the myths and maps of psychology, we shall want to tell the story of God's people in pilgrimage and growth. We shall have some signposts and some guidelines from the pages of Scripture to help us in the work of counselling and gossiping the gospel.

Furthermore, such a high view of Scripture will demand a high view of the sacraments—especially the Eucharist, Baptism, and Healing—as signs of the gospel record at work in the flesh and blood lives of our contemporary church. In public reading of the Scriptures, we shall take care to do this well and with a sense of awe. We shall recognize that such a ministry of reading the Scriptures in worship demands a special charism and gifts of grace. The Scriptures will be read with awe and listened to with attention and with a sense of expectation. This approach to the Scriptures will change the whole climate of the liturgy of the word in our worship and indeed it will change our whole expectation as the preacher mounts the steps of the pulpit.

In our interaction with the secular culture of our age, where we know we are being brainwashed daily with prejudices and presuppositions, the Christian will have a resource in the Scriptures that is powerful to frame and fashion what Harry Blamires has called the Christian mind. The Christian disciple, armed with a deep knowledge of and love for the Scriptures will be competent to take the Bible in one hand and the newspaper in the other and to engage the latter with the critique of the former as well as the other way round. But above all, the Bible will be our personal daily nurture. Must not the Bible be our daily companion? Richard Lovelace writes:

> The Christian who wants to encounter God without listening to what he has to say may remain in the condition of a singularly sub-literate and disobedient two-year-old. Sanctification of the mind is of pivotal importance in sanctification of the whole life and sanctification of the mind involves an increasing ability to think biblically under the empowering of the spirit.[29]

Notes

1. Stephen Neill, *Anglicanism* (Harmondsworth: Penguin, 1958).
2. R. H. Lightfoot, *History and Interpretation in the Gospels* (Hodder & Stoughton, London, 1935) p. 225.
3. D. E. Nineham and others, *History and Chronology in the New Testament* (SPCK, London, 1965) p. 4.
4. Basil Willey, *History, Criticism and Faith*, Ed. Colin Brown (Inter-Varsity Press, 1976) p. 106.
5. *The Meaning of Persons* (Harper & Row, 1973), pp. 162–163.
6. Thomas Merton, *Seven Storey Mountain* (First Harvest-HBJ, 1978), p. 293.
7. Peter Moore, Paper given at Winter Park Conference, 1986.
8. 2 Timothy 3:16.
9. 1 Peter 1:23ff.
10. 1 Thessalonians 2:13.
11. 1 Corinthians 2:13.
12. Matthew 5:17f.
13. John 10:35.
14. John 5:39, 40.
15. Frederick Buechner, *Wishful Thinking* (New York: Harper and Row, 1973), p. 12.
16. Luke 2:19.
17. Luke 24:32.
18. Karl Barth, *The Word of God and the Word of Men* (New York: Harper Torch Books, 1957) p. 63.
19. Isaiah 7:14.
20. Genesis 18:9ff.
21. 1 Samuel 1.
22. 1 Samuel 2:1ff.
23. Luke 1:46ff.
24. See 1 Samuel 9:21.
25. Luke 24:5.
26. Frederick Buechner, op. cit., p. 6.
27. Mark 13:14.
28. Acts 4:20.
29. Richard Lovelace, *Dynamics of Spiritual Life* (Inter-Varsity Press, 1979).

SEVEN

We Have a Gospel to Proclaim

THE CHURCH AND THE GOSPEL

Some time ago, at a clergy conference convened by the clergy for the clergy in the name and with the purpose of renewal, some of those present were sharing their disappointments and frustrations in their ministry. There were soul-searching comments and honest appraisal. One priest—a man of prayer, thought, and deep pastoral experience over many years, recounted how he had taken great trouble throughout his ministry to spend a lot of hours in counseling couples preparing for marriage. Sadly, he concluded that this long and careful counseling seldom issued in regular and committed membership of the church. The group was largely catholic in churchmanship, though such labels were not in evidence for purposes of the discussion. At one point, another member of the group asked the priest to share with the rest of those present the kind of things he might say to couples about their need for faith. "Well," he replied, "I ask them quite directly. 'Wouldn't you like the church to be part of your new life together and your family to be part of the wider family of the church?'"

Not bad, you might think. But that is *not* how St. Paul commended membership in the church. Membership in the church and commitment to the church in the New Testament issued out

of a living faith in Jesus Christ. "You are the Christ, the son of
the living God."[1] "Yes, Peter, and that is the kind of faith on
which my church is built," replies Jesus. Confession of faith issues
in commitment to the church and the church is built and founded
upon apostolic witness. That priest—and I want to insist that he
was a good priest—had allowed the primacy of the gospel and the
unique place of Jesus Christ who is Lord of Scripture and also
Lord of his church, somehow to slip out of his vocabulary and
was relying upon the institution and family of the church (important though they are) to do what they simply are not competent to do. It was the clergy at the Winter Park Conference
who shared this concern in their own ministry, permitting such
slippage to occur when they said "We, who are in the ordained
ministry, have compromised our witness through ignorance of the
scriptures, deliberate conformity to the world and failure to profess
and confess the lordship of Christ."[2] And so in their turn one of
the groups at that same conference was compelled to admit that
too many people in the Episcopal Church "come to adulthood
without being challenged to commit their lives to Jesus as savior
and lord."

Of course the church is important as the corporate expression
of faith in Jesus Christ. Of course the sacraments show forth
Christ's saving work effectively in the lives of those who partake
in the celebration. However, there is nothing uncatholic and at
the same time there is something essentially scriptural about specifically witnessing to Jesus Christ as Lord and Savior. Read some
of the sermons of the great Anglo-Catholic leaders of renewal in
England at the close of the nineteenth century and the beginning
of the twentieth century: Stanton, Macchonochie, and Mackay.
They are biblical sermons. They are evangelistic sermons. There
you will find that they frequently speak of Jesus and that they are
not ashamed to have an altar-call at the climax of their presentations. The preaching of these men brought ordinary men and
women to know Jesus Christ and to love him with all their mind,
with all their heart and with all their passions. There was incense
and ceremonial in their services. There was color in their vest-
ments and beauty in the music of the liturgy. But at the same

time there was the presence of Jesus in the Word in the pulpit as well as in the Bread at the altar and there was the judgment as well as the compassion of Christ in their confessionals. They sang in processions with candles, cross, and chasubles, but there was no mistake about the message that issued forth from these some-what exuberant ecclesiastical extravaganzas. "All for Jesus"—that is what they were singing in those churches and outside in the poor streets of the large industrial and poor cities of England. "All for Jesus, all for Jesus, that shall be the church's song."[3] Somewhere in his ministry we feel compelled to reflect that that good priest had lost the essential content of the gospel and was carrying round in his ministry the burden of a cause, a commu-nity, and a church.

Perhaps he never got it right at the very outset of his ministry because the church as an institution was given first place in his seminary syllabus. He learned how to say Mass (at least that is how he would refer to it in his tradition). He learned about the history of the church and was fired by its story, its heroism, and its witness in the so-called ages of faith. He learned how to hear confessions and swallowed a great deal incidentally in recent years about counseling. In the Bible parts of the syllabus however, he spent more time reading books about the Bible than actually reading the Bible itself. The books he read about the Bible led him to feel uneasy about its authority, accuracy, or its dependa-bility. And so in short, he left the seminary equipped to head up an institution (the parish). He was determined to live the life of a Christian and to try to say his prayers and care for the people committed to his care.

But he had not been *gospelled* or, to put it another way, he had not been "newed," let alone renewed! For one thing emerges very clearly in any gathering of renewal. Something necessarily has to happen to people in addition to their baptism, confirma-tion, or seminary training and ordination at some point (or at various points) in their subsequent pilgrimage if they are "daily to increase in his Holy Spirit more and more"[4] until they come to his eternal kingdom. It is misleading to call these various ex-periences by the name of "baptism" in the Spirit. It is misguided to set up any one of the gifts of the Spirit as goals or models for Christian discipleship—except love as expounded by St. Paul in 1 Corinthians 13. Nevertheless, it has to be said that into the static once-and-for-all of baptism and confirmation (or ordination) there must be the dynamic of the Spirit which promotes discipleship, journeying, pilgrimage, conversion, and deepening of faith and conviction. As the church emerges from Christendom and begins by reflection to look more and more like the church of the New Testament before Christendom began, the lines of faith, conversion, and commitment to Jesus Christ will become more and more evident, and faith will need in its turn to become more and more articulate.

This of course makes new demands upon ministry in its widest sense, as well as upon the ordained ministry in particular. In the years ahead we are going to need more and more evangelists. We are going to need more and more teachers who are more than just counselors. We are going to need catechists and not so many people writing books about Christianity, as more Christians writing books about the thousand and one other issues which need to be faced with the challenge of the gospel. We are going to need Christian minds informed by the disciplines of economics, science, biology, and politics, to name but a few. In many ways the church needs an army equipped for battle on the frontiers of conflicting outlooks where in the past it resembled much more the life style and gentle manners of a country club quietly recruiting for membership.

So we need to rehearse again and again the content of our gospel—and furthermore a gospel which clearly has the power to save. For the times are urgent and the days are evil. Do the mainstream churches in fact today have a gospel that is powerful enough to save? Or are we too bland and too genteel to speak to an age which is living on the edge of a precipice? For the liberal and the renaissance man have not been to the edge of that precipice and looked into the abyss of self-destruction. They have not discovered that grace and grace alone in the end is powerful enough to pull fallen man back from the edge of disaster. Such apparently self-sufficient souls have not experienced at first hand

the terrible destruction of drugs, alcohol, AIDS, or what Richard
Holloway calls erotomania.[5] Their temptation is always to substitute bland ecclesiastical rhetoric for salvation preaching. They will
be embarrassed by the testimony of a brutal slave trader who could
write after his conversion the words of a wonderful hymn because
he first experienced those words in the bowels of his suffering and
degradation: "Amazing grace! how sweet the sound that saved a
wretch like me."[6] They will all too easily draw back from such
absolutes and such crossroads until the kingdom of God is blandly
conceived as involving "no discontinuities, no crises; no trage-
dies, or sacrifices, no loss of all things, no Cross and Resurrection."[7] Speaking of this trend in American liberal protestantism,
Richard Niebuhr summed up this whole movement in the church
in the following devastating words:

> In ethics, it [liberal protestantism] reconciles the interests of
> the individual with those of society, by means of faith in a
> natural identity of interests or in the benevolent, altruistic
> character of man. In politics and economics it slurred over
> national and class divisions, seeing only the growth of unity
> and ignoring the increase of self-assertion and exploitation.
> In religion it reconciled God and man by deifying the latter
> and humanizing the former . . . Christ the redeemer became
> Jesus the teacher or the spiritual genius in whom the religious
> capacities of mankind were fully developed . . . evolution,
> growth, development, the culture of the religious life, the
> nurture of the kindly sentiments, the extension of humani-
> tarian ideals, and the progress of civilization all took the
> place of the Christian revolution . . . a God without wrath
> brought men without sin into a kingdom without judgement
> through the ministrations of a Christ without a Cross.

It is the contention of this book that the erosion of the Episcopal
church by that kind of perversion of the saving gospel of Jesus
Christ is at the root of death in the Episcopal church today. Such
a perversion renders the gospel and the church powerless to bring
healing and restoration to the souls of broken men and women.
That good priest described at the start of this chapter was bearing
testimony to the failure of anything less than full-blooded apos-

tolic, catholic, and scriptural Christianity. The crisis for the church today is neither one which will be solved in a cosmetic face-lift for the church, nor in a concern for new causes. The crisis for the church today is a crisis of content of belief. What do we believe? What is our gospel?

THE CONTENT OF THE GOSPEL: WORD AND SACRAMENT

The liturgical movement, important though it has been, is impotent in itself to bring souls to Jesus Christ. All right, we now have a new Prayer Book and new hymnal. Two cheers! But let no one suppose that cosmetics and liturgical renewal in themselves are going to bring renewal to the church. Equally there are many important issues and causes facing the church and rightly demanding our attention. But in themselves, and left to themselves they have the destructive power to reduce Christianity to just another ideology, providing only a booth and sideshow in the circus of competing ideologies at a General Convention. The crisis for the Episcopal Church is quite simply this—what do we believe? The crisis for every individual Christian within our church (ordained or lay) could be summed up in this way: what do I believe? If you were waiting to be shot tomorrow morning in a terrorist camp, would you have something to say about Jesus Christ that you simply felt compelled to say to the prisoner waiting in the cell next door to you? The times are as urgent as that, and the challenge is as poignant as that—even for Episcopalians and not just for Baptists or extreme sectarians.

In the Episcopal church in particular and in Anglicanism in general, we are committed to word and sacrament: two methods of effectively presenting a single gospel. The sacraments of the church are intended to be actions speaking far louder than words, yet telling us through all our senses the same saving truths of the same gospel that we hear preached with power from the pulpit or read with conviction and rapt attention from the pages of Scripture in the course of the liturgy. In a word, we need to *gospelize* the sacraments and to *sacramentalize* the gospel. And that word if it had to be summed up in a single phrase could well be the words we so often see painted on cliff sides, on bridges over highways, or indeed in all sorts of unexpected places by religious nutters: Jesus saves. Jesus saves, because God loves. That is the heart of the revelation which we call gospel—good news.

How do we know God loves? We cannot discern this from our newspapers. We cannot discern this from the evidence of the jungle of creation. We can only know it because it has been revealed to us: it is, in a word, saving knowledge. We do not get that knowledge simply by thinking a lot, speculating a lot, or by looking at the created order around us. For, in fact, there is much in that created order with all its suffering that might suggest that if there is a God he is either incompetent or indifferent. But revelation has a word for us: Jesus saves because God loves. We have a word from God that tells us that in spite of evidence to the contrary, there is a God. But more than that, He loves and he longs to save. That is revelation and not mere speculation. "In many and various ways God spoke of old to our fathers by the prophets: but in these last days he has spoken to us by a son."[8] "Inscribed upon the Cross we see in shining letters: God is love."[9] Or in the words of Karl Barth, the great theologian, reducing all his dogmatics to the simplicity of a childlike affirmation: "Jesus loves me, this I know, for the Bible tells me so."[10]

The corporate witness of the church in its preaching and its sacraments is to reassure us of this reality as the once-and-for-all declaration by God in his word of the gospel and in the good news made flesh in Jesus Christ. He has said it once-and-for-all on Calvary: "Father, forgive them for they know not what they do."[11] A more accurate translation of that text in St. Luke would suggest by its two parallel imperfect tenses that Jesus did not say these words once only. He kept on saying those words as fast as they were knocking in the nails. Perhaps a more accurate translation might read—"as they were crucifying him, Jesus kept on saying, 'Father forgive, Father forgive.' "

So once-and-for-all in our baptism we are forgiven. We are made regenerate. That is the rock of our confidence: our baptism into this Jesus who saves. But what does St. Thomas Aquinas say?

"God does not need the sacraments: we do." So in actions which speak far louder than words, and in many different ways and at many varying points on the road of our discipleship, we need to recall and make present for ourselves the once-and-for-all sacrament of our baptism into Christ. "Look not us, but look on us as found in him."[12] Sinners we are; yet reckoned righteous. In other words, Jesus saves. It is almost as though we need the sign language of the sacraments to spell out to the human race which is half deaf, half blind, and half dumb, and half daft, that God in reality loves us. The sign language for the deaf is a very concrete language. As for the deaf through their signs, the sacraments are intended to address us in a concrete language and through all our senses but at the same time they are intended to convey the power and content of the preached word that can be summarized in those words painted in all the most unlikely places of our world: Jesus saves.

Perhaps the most powerful of these sacramental signs occurs at Easter, in the vigil celebration focused as it is around the death and resurrection of Jesus and the sacramental re-presentation of that reality in the sacrament of baptism. The new Christians are baptized into the death and resurrection of Jesus which is celebrated at every level of sensitivity and consciousness in the life of the church on that most Holy Night. The rest of the Christians are made new as they align with the new Christians in re-affirming their baptismal vows, getting into step, and then celebrating the death and resurrection of Jesus in the Easter Eucharist. That is where the corporate, sacramental, and institutional renewal of the church is focused each year around the font. Ideally this should be done with the bishop present, witnessing in a truly apostolic way to the resurrection of Jesus, at work in the very heart and life of his body, the church—that church that is itself a sacramental sign of the dying and rising of Jesus.

In all of this it must be freely admitted that the new Prayer Book is indeed a helpful bonus. Nevertheless, that Prayer Book is essentially a resource book and not a pew book. We really do have to ask ourselves a serious question about the Prayer Book, pastorally. If we want it to be used in the churches in such a way that still anticipates the presence of new worshippers, then it is essential that at every service the whole of the service is printed out in pamphlet form and in such a way that commends itself to easy use by the uninitiated. Yet the Prayer Book in the Episcopal church is indeed a bonus once we acknowledge that it cannot do all that has to be done for our church if our worship is to be *gospelled* afresh and if the life of the church is to be on the frontier where new Christians are being formed and where new members are attending. The clergy who use it in their turn must hold gospel convictions in order to help them to tailor the worship in such a way that it really does present effectively the gospel and make it real for those who are worshipping, even worshipping perhaps for the first time.

Furthermore, counseling and advice in pastoral care are not enough. We have a gospel to proclaim in that setting as well. The sensitive and gospelled pastor will know when it is right to stop giving advice and begin to pray. Those prayers will be addressed, furthermore, to a God who acts, and who is expected to act today as he did in Jesus two thousand years ago. Salvation means healing. In place of the word salvation in our ecclesiastical vocabulary and in most modern translations of the Scripture, Tyndale in his first translation of the Bible into English put the word health or healing. Furthermore, Jesus puts forgiveness and healing together in the same passage in the miracle of healing at Capernaum in St. Mark's gospel.[13] The Sacraments are intended to be signs of that healing at work today. They are signs of the kingdom at work in a church and through a ministry anointed by the power of the Holy Spirit. It is the same Holy Spirit that anointed Jesus for the same salvation ministry that we read about in St. Luke's gospel:

> The spirit of the Lord is upon me, because he has anointed me to preach good news to the poor. He has sent me to proclaim release to the captives and recovering of sight to the blind, to set at liberty those who are oppressed, to proclaim the acceptable year of the Lord."[14]

Word and Sacraments together should recall the church to its essential identity (a school for disciples, a hospital for sinners and a hospice for the dying). Word and Sacrament together must enable the church to celebrate these saving acts of Christ in the lives of those who are summoned by the Word and gathered together for worship. Then, and then only, the church becomes a sign of the gospel and the power of Christ to save and to heal the lives of men and women in every generation.

Expectation, joy, and obedience characterize such a church. Worship and other services become events of expectation and the fellowship of the faithful becomes an environment for healing and salvation. In a word, Jesus saves. The church is then seen as the theater where the divine drama is continually acted out and where we witness to the death and resurrection of Jesus because we have first participated in that divine event and known it to be saving truth for ourselves. For the death and resurrection of Jesus is the turning point in the cosmic history of the universe, and it is indeed under God and by his grace the property and responsibility of the church. We are stewards of these saving mysteries.[15]

THE PRIORITY OF PREACHING

All this places a particular responsibility on the church to give a proper place to the word in its worship. It has to be said that the recovery of the Eucharist as the characteristic act of Christian worship for the Lord's people on the Lord's day, in the Episcopal church has had two accompanying detrimental effects. In the first place, it has quenched the spirit of preaching and diminished the stature of the Word in services that are exclusively services of the Eucharist. If they are not exclusively services of the Eucharist, it tends to mean nevertheless that the Sacrament dominates the word. Sermonettes make Christianettes. Ten minutes from the chancel steps will simply not do. St. Augustine speaks of the banquet of the word. Fast food cannot sustain and build up God's people.

Second, we have to acknowledge that in a culture that seems to permit only one visit to church on a Sunday by the faithful (which is generally expected to last no longer than one hour) there is no opportunity for good preaching at non-Eucharistic services in most Episcopal churches today. We have, by our eucharistic obsession unchurched whole parts of America and sent them to good Bible-preaching services outside the Episcopal church. We desperately need to recover in Anglicanism, mission, and evangelistic services either seasonally on six Sundays in Lent, four Sundays in Advent, or perhaps the six weeks after Easter. Such services could take place on Sunday evenings, or afternoons, somewhere, somehow, and at some time, so that the word—and especially the evangelistic opportunity and responsibility for that word—is not lost. It was Archbishop Basil Hume who said of the Roman Catholic community in England that they were oversacramentalized and underevangelized. The same has to be said for many parts of the Episcopal church today.

Yet all this will require a new commitment to the word of Scripture and to the priority of preaching in our churches. There is no longer the need to polarize word and Sacraments. They are both intended to be powerful means of gospel proclamation, celebration, and presentation in the life of the church and in the discipleship of the faithful. The commitment to the craft and charism of preaching is time consuming for a minister of the word. Having recovered our confidence in the Scriptures (and that is the first step, but generally a step taken for most ministers *after* seminary days rather than during them), the minister of the Word must then turn to the Bible and make it a lifetime study. The Bible is the living proclamation of God's saving power in the history of his people. With it God gives to the church the joyful task and awesome responsibility of preaching. He makes that same saving power available today through the preached word. Preaching is an event—not an essay. We must mount the pulpit steps with awe and expectation—"Today, if you will hear his voice."[16] Something is going to happen! The blind will begin to see, the deaf will begin to hear, and the lame will begin to walk. Each and every sermon must be cruciform in shape, bringing its hearers to Calvary Hill, to the foot of the Cross, proclaiming forgiveness, healing, and new life, and pointing through judgment to acquittal, release, and that new life in the kingdom. The preacher must

have known perforce in his own life that saving power as surely
as only a recovered alcoholic who has taken that first step can
speak to another alcoholic in need about the possibility of true
sobriety. He has a story to tell, and therefore, he has a life to live.
He will not point to fruits until he has established roots. There
will be no moralism, no palagianism, no mere exhorting to the
good life. In a word there will be some old-fashioned gospel
preaching bringing people to a point of decision and to something
of an altar-call expressed sacramentally.

And all this because the preacher is primarily a person who
lives under the yoke of Scripture; in a word, a biblical person
whose whole outlook and perspective upon life has been fashioned
by daily study of the Scriptures. Where there is a preacher there
is a living church and in its turn a living church will always raise
up and demand a preacher. For "how are men to call upon him
in whom they have not believed? And how are they to believe in
him of whom they have never heard? And how are they to hear
without a preacher?"[17] This affirmation of the important place of
the word in the life of the church should no longer be a question
of churchmanship. It is perhaps in this area of salvation theology
that most in the name of unity has been achieved in recent years.
Evangelicals and catholics, refreshed and renewed by the Holy
Spirit, have converged upon the need for a clearly presented and
powerful gospel which has both a cutting edge with the emergency
of surgery as well as the balm of healing and reconciliation for
growth and long-term discipleship.

Even the sacrament of reconciliation, proclaimed and celebrated in the environment of pastoral counseling and rooted in
the power of the word, proclaimed as good news for this person
at this point on their pilgrimage (and frequently accompanied
with prayer and laying on of hands), need no longer be seen as
divisive or as the slogan and practice of one particular party
within the church.

We have a gospel to proclaim. Woe to us if we do not proclaim
that gospel, by word and deed, by Scripture and Sacrament, in
season and out of season. Wherever and whenever we do just that
in obedience and empowered by the Holy Spirit, there the church

is renewed, because Jesus is raised up and God is glorified in his church.

And this in its turn will result in apostolic witness. The gospel will be gossiped, simply because what is happening in the life of the church will be impossible to suppress. "We cannot but speak of what we have seen and heard." The club mentality of the ecclesiastical institution will be replaced by an explosive spirit that no upper room can possibly any longer contain. In America the doors of all public buildings open outward in case of fire. That should be, by grace, a mandate for all churches. Our doors only open outward, but not in case of fire, but precisely because of fire—the fire of Pentecost. Every believer is called to apostolic witness. As surely as a recovering alcoholic is not ashamed to tell his story, so the Christian believer, male and female, ordained or lay, should never be ashamed to tell their story: "I will tell you what the Lord has done for my soul."

The proper translation of the title of the book in the New Testament—the book of the Acts of the Apostles—would more correctly be (in the absence in the Greek of two definite articles) "a record of apostolic acts." That is what the church should be— a kind of soap opera of apostolic acts, making up the continued and continual drama of God's saving acts at work in the everyday lives of everyday believers. There is a real need to recapture (rather than to return to) or perhaps to be recaptured by, the spirit of the church as we see it outlined in that record of apostolic acts. Further, there is frankly (and this has to be freely admitted by the church today), a new urgency to change the life-style of Christians from individualism to corporate community, from affluence and acquisitiveness to simplicity, generosity, and hospitality. For the first Christians held all things in common. We cannot continue to live with a credibility gap between the words of the message and the life-style of the messengers. "We desire to return to the basics of the apostolic faith—preaching, teaching, and holiness of life. We invite our brothers and sisters of the church to stand with us in fear and trembling knowing that to this our Lord has called us and for this he holds us accountable."[18]

Notes

1. Mark 8:29.
2. Quotation from Winter Park Conference, 1986 Statement.
3. Stainer, *Crucifixion.*
4. See Confirmation Prayer, *Book of Common Prayer,* 1662.
5. See Richard Holloway, *Suffering, Sex and Other Paradoxes* (Wilton, Conn.: Morehouse-Barlow, 1984), chapter four.
6. John Newton, "Amazing Grace!" *The Hymnal 1982,* No. 671.
7. H. Richard Niebuhr, *The Kingdom of God in America* (New York: Harper Torchbook, date), pp. 191ff.
8. Hebrews 1:1f.
9. Charles William Everest, "Take up your cross," *The Hymnal 1982,* No. 675.
10. Karl Barth, *Dogmatics.*
11. Luke 23:34.
12. William Bright, "And now, O Father, mindful of the love," *The Hymnal 1982,* No. 337.
13. Mark 2.
14. Luke 4:18.
15. See 1 Corinthians 4:1.
16. Psalms 95:8.
17. Romans 10:14.
18. Quotation from Winter Park Conference, 1986 Statement.

EIGHT

The Church as Life in the Spirit

THE FORMULA OF EVANGELISM

"They continued steadfastly in the apostles' doctrine, the fellowship, the breaking of bread and prayer."[1] After the first blast of Pentecost, and when the apostolic thrust and dust had settled somewhat, in that one verse, Luke summarizes something of what the first shoots of the tender, newborn church looked like on the landscape of history. (Come to think of it, it was not such a very small plant; in fact, we are told that there were over three thousand in number of those first new Christians.)[2] However, this new church sprang straight out of apostolic preaching. It is Peter who witnesses to the Resurrection of Jesus. This preaching in its turn leads to repentance and baptism, and all in the same bundle the promise of the gift of the Holy Spirit. On that day alone, we are told, "about three thousand" received God's word from the lips of Peter. Again and again in very different strata and on the lips of very different witnesses, we find this same expression "receiving the word." It involves so much more, of course, than just the process of hearing the Word. It is that interiorizing of the Word of which we have spoken earlier and of which Jesus speaks in St. John's gospel.[3]

It is this combination of events that forms the church. First apostolic preaching, which is essentially witnessing to the Resurrection of Jesus; then the challenge to receive the Word; repentance; baptism; the gift of the Holy Spirit; "And there were added that day about three thousand souls." *That is the formula for evangelism.* That is the formula for building up the church. There is nothing new in it, nothing requiring special human talent. It is primarily God's work and God's activity carried out in the lives of men and women who acknowledge the lordship of Christ in all things and who are seeking to do his will with obedient and loving hearts. But above all, it is always essentially the same message on the lips of those who bear apostolic witness—Jesus and the resurrection. Wherever these ingredients are present, there we find new Christians and there we find Christians being made new. In a word, it is there that we find the church, and it is a church in renewal.

But the church we find is not primarily perceived either as an organization or an institution. Pentecost does not resemble in any way an annual general meeting! Our attention is soon drawn away from the strange and awesome pentecostal signs of wind and fire. Our gaze now fastens upon a crowd of men and women who are living unselfconsciously in the life of that same Holy Spirit, but in a very down-to-earth and practical way. Their lives seem to have a pattern, a rhythm, and a shape. "They continued steadfastly"; this Pentecost business is no flash in the pan. It is a whole new way of life, but lived in the old and only way you can ever live life in this world—one day at a time. What we are witnessing in Luke's rather careful, even meticulous account of the emergence of the church in history, is the drawing together of bands and cells of men and women living the life of the spirit. Their conversion summons them to a corporate commitment to live out the life of Christ in a body, a cell, a group. There is no self-conscious individualism or pietism in these early chapters, except perhaps the rather shocking incident of the individualism of Ananias and Sapphira; and we know what happened to them! "Now the company of those who believed" (that is another way in which Luke describes the infant church) "were of one heart and soul, and no one said that any of the things which he possessed was his own, but they had everything in common . . . there was not a needy person among them, for as many as were possessors of land or houses sold them, and brought the proceeds of what was sold and laid it at the apostles' feet; and distribution was made to each as any had need."[4]

Of course, this passage is today frequently abused by many who would want to make a straight equation between primitive Christianity and Communism or even Marxism. Even worse, it is often absurdly suggested that here we have the first crop of budding little socialists. Nothing could be further from the truth. Right in the center of this passage, there is verse thirty-three, which is what changes the whole chemistry of these verses, and it is this verse and all that it implies that is so often conspicuously missing among those who seek to build self-styled communities or who try to impose the political ideology of socialism upon the shape and features of the early church. "And with great power the apostles gave their testimony to the Resurrection of the Lord Jesus."[5] (Here it is again—Jesus and his Resurrection.) But notice now what Luke adds. Issuing straight out of that powerful apostolic preaching he records, "Great grace was upon them all."[6] Here it is for the very first time in volume two of St. Luke. Amazing grace! Grace—God's amazing generosity. Undeserved, unearned, unattainable—showered, generous to the point of apparent wastefulness and prodigality. Of course, they are not getting what they deserve; the economy of the kingdom does not work that way. For it is the economy of the kingdom which we are witnessing here breaking into the life of the church, and it brings with it an amazing awareness of what God has done and continues to do for them. Their response is inevitable. Thanksgiving and Eucharist spill over as they must do and always to and for others. Also with an absurd Godlike generosity, there is apparent wastefulness and prodigality. And all this is because they know that this is what God has done for *them*. Freely have they received, freely they can give.

> Were the whole realm of nature mine,
> That were an offering far too small;

Love so amazing, so divine,
Demands my soul, my life, my all.[7]

That is why Ananias and Sapphira have no place in the economy of this newly formed community. Grace cannot be cool and calculating in that way. So St. Paul later works out the full implications, politically, economically, and ecclesiastically in his treatise on the interdependence of the body in his first Epistle to the Corinthians. The body does not consist of one member but of many. If the foot should say "because I am not a hand, I do not belong to the body," that would not make it any less a part of the body.[8] In other words, there is no room for individualism or for competition. On the contrary it is *interdependence* that marks the corporate life of the body of the church. No one member lives for himself, but for the body. "If one member suffers, all suffer together. If one member is honored, all rejoice together."[9] No one needs to try and neither should anyone try in this new economy to get by on his or her own. Ananias and Sapphira are severely out of step. "The eye cannot say to the hand, 'I have no need of you,' nor again the head to the feet, 'I have no need of you.' "[10]

Metaphorically, in the power struggles of our society today, both economically and politically, that is precisely what the head is saying to the hand: "I have no need of you." The mental and the manual workers are alienated and competitive. Our whole educational system is aimed at helping people to "get ahead," and implies the superiority of workers who use their head over those who use their hands: the white-collar worker versus the blue-collar worker.

Now the early church in contradiction to society's power struggles (just as evident in Rome in the first century as in New York in the twentieth century) was raised up as a sign of contradiction to all of this. It was raised up to be a sign of the new kingdom. The church was to be itself evidence of this new way of life. It would turn its back on the old regime of every man for himself and begin to live as every man for others. But it did not do this in a self-conscious or self-righteous way. It certainly did

not do it in an individualistic way. It was graced. It saw itself as
the victim of incredible generosity: God's generosity—nothing
less than amazing grace. Furthermore, the Holy Spirit's first concern is to form the body by breaking down what divides and by
reforming the stuctures into a new and transcendent unity. The
Spirit forms the body: the Holy Spirit forms the body of Christ
in the world (the church) as surely as by the overshadowing of
Mary, he formed the body of Christ in Mary's womb.

All this is what St. Luke observes in that first brief description
of the work and life of the Spirit in the apostolic church. Furthermore, in this church as life in the Spirit develops and grows
out of faithfulness to a ministry of Word and Sacrament, it ac-
knowledges the Lordship of Christ and is empowered by the same
Holy Spirit.

> They devoted themselves to the apostles' teaching and fel-
> lowship, to the breaking of bread and the prayers. And fear
> came upon every soul; and many wonders and signs were done
> through the apostles. And all who believed were together
> and had all things in common; and they sold their possessions
> and goods and distributed them to all, as any had need. And
> day by day, attending the temple together and breaking bread
> in their houses, they partook of food with glad and generous
> hearts, praising God and having favor with all the people.
> And the Lord added to their number day by day those who
> were being saved. [11]

We need to study this passage in great detail, so that we can
begin to see the characteristics of this early and Spirit-filled
church. In other words, we need to observe what happens when
we get behind the church viewed primarily as an institution and
into a church that is essentially a band of men and women living
in the life of the Spirit. Such an experience should not lead us
to suppose that we can go back in history and live in a non-
institutionalized church. You cannot go back into history that
way or indeed in any other way, and in one sense, you will never
have a church in time that is not in some sense institutionalized.
The object of this exercise is very different. It is based upon the
conviction that the institution cannot renew the institution. The

only force capable of renewing an insitution is the original force that created that institution. We take the institution in its contemporary manifestation and make sure that all the original ingredients are present and evident. The outward facade may or may not change radically. That depends upon many factors. Our main concern will not be with externals, which may vary in coloring, shape, size, and style according to the culture and age in which the church is called upon to serve. Our first and fundamental concern is with the inner life of the church, making sure that all those first apostolic ingredients for a healthy church are still there. It is in that spirit that we go to the task of our Bible study on life in the Spirit in the church of the apostolic age.

ESSENTIAL CHARACTERISTICS IN THE CHURCH OF THE APOSTOLIC AGE

In the first place we find that it was a learning church. They continued persistently, regularly, and steadfastly to listen to the teaching of the Apostles. We know the Apostles spent a great deal of their time preaching and proclaiming the gospel—the good news of Jesus and his resurrection. That *kerygma* was a distinctive message and by reading carefully the New Testament in general and the book of the Acts of the Apostles in particular, we can see that it was not long before "the message" became well defined and itself almost institutionalized. They could soon tell the story of Jesus's Resurrection and the saving acts of God by rote.

But in addition to that sort of preaching of the message, there was the daily teaching responsibility that was laid upon the shoulders of the Apostles and in their turn the commitment of the new disciples to be taught and trained in the full meaning of their new-found faith. Here was persistent and consistent teaching and training for the whole church and not mere trivial pursuits in useless ecclesiastical gossip. These new converts needed to be fed, sustained, and edified, and above all to grow in the understanding of their faith until they could say with St. Paul that they had the mind of Christ. We need in our churches today more and more

teaching and training of this kind: education and inspiration in
consistent programs for Christians at all stages of their discipleship: pre-baptism and confirmation; post-confirmation and pre-
marriage instruction.

This whole program needs to go right the way through from
the cradle to the grave, learning how to live the Christian life;
learning how to die in order that we may live for ever. This is
not primarily a cerebral process though it will certainly include
some mind-stretching experiences. It cannot all be done (and
neither should it be) from the pulpit. If it cannot be done on
evenings during the week (for apparently Episcopalians do not go
out at all during the week in the evenings!), it must be done as
part of the Sunday morning program. Perhaps we need to extend
occasionally the whole of the Sunday morning program to include
a teaching program and even a parish lunch together. In season
and out of season, the church must be a learning church, but
perhaps especially during Lent and Eastertide when the church
can gather around the new Christians and go to school in the
mysteries of Jesus, his death and his resurrection. That message
of Jesus and his resurrection needs to be expounded, evangelized,
celebrated, and sacramentalized with witness and worship to the
point where it is totally interiorized by all those who partake in
the celebration. Only in this way will the body of Christ be built
up. We need more and more teaching and preaching ministry.
Yet where the church takes its teaching and preaching program
seriously, there the body of Christ is indeed built up, because at
all points of our discipleship and life in the Spirit we must be
visibly challenged to be a learning church.

But the church is also a church of fellowship in the Spirit. It
enjoys a common life, not because it is a group of like-minded
people who happen to get on rather well together. On the contrary, the church is not a freemasonry of like-minded people at
all. It is a community of very differing characters (the good, the
bad, and the indifferent) who have been dislocated and called out
by the Holy Spirit from any form of self-sufficiency and thrown
together by that same Holy Spirit in the largest experiment in

community life our evolution has ever witnessed. That is what is meant by the church being truly catholic.

So there will be nothing hearty or back-slapping about this business of fellowship. We see in verses forty-four and forty-five of Acts 2 that this church was a sharing church, but sharing at every level. They shared their goods and their strengths. They also shared their suffering and their weaknesses. It was said that William Morris never saw a drunken man without feeling a personal responsibility for him. This *koinonia* of the Spirit, far from grouping us into a clique, turns us around to stand together and face outward to all the pressures and the sufferings that surround us. Yet above all it is this same Holy Spirit who in obedience to Christ's command challenges the Christian church locally to that most difficult of all experiments: to love *one another*. It is easy to love the world in general. It is much more difficult to love the person in the pew next to me. After all I did not choose to be next to this particular person and of course this particular person did not choose to be next to me. The church is not a self-selecting community. Therefore Christ's command to love one another is necessarily the baseline of his further example and challenge to love and to care for the world at large.

As we continue in our Bible study we discover that the church was also essentially a praying church. "They always went into God before they went out to the world; they were able to meet the problems of life because they had first met him."[12] They lived by prayer because they lived by faith in God who provided. It meant that they could afford to take risks, because they were drawing upon a strength beyond anything that they possessed naturally. Intercession was not just a way of prayer; it was a whole way of life, a life lived for others as well as a way of praying for others. Intercession is a Latin legal word which means literally to go into the judge on behalf of someone else. We shall see later in this book that such a life (as well as such prayers) is essentially a mark of the priestly life. They learned this about prayer, but they learned more. They learned a certain quality of prayer of the heart St. Paul describes as praying at all times.[13] Even more than this, it meant that they prayed together as well as for each other. But in all of this, there was that childlike simplicity of heart which takes a father at his word and relies upon that word in every way. "Ask and you shall receive, seek and you shall find, knock and the door will be opened."[14] They were testing their doctrine in their prayer experience and in its turn, that prayer experience endorsed their doctrine about all the gifts that God gave them in everyday life.

Of course it was a sacramental church also where believers were baptized and where they broke bread daily from house to house. And all this is part of their worship for which they came together knowing that by the Holy Spirit, Jesus was made present to them as their risen and glorified Lord at the heart of his church whenever they came together. It was when they came together in this way (or rather in his way, the way he had told them to) it was then, that so often things happened—those signs and wonders of which Acts 2:43 speaks so eloquently. They expected great things to happen, because whenever God and man come together (Emmanuel) all things are possible.[15] They had, quite literally, great expectations! Their corporate life was itself daily evidence of the power of the gospel at work among them, playing the same old record and endorsing the same old message: the blind were seeing, the lame were walking, and the deaf were hearing, and even the poor were receiving the good news.

This was the experience then of the church living in the life of the Spirit. That life formed itself into a daily corporate life of apostolic teaching, fellowship, breaking of bread, and prayer. It happened then and it happens still. It happens still if those who go to church are not just churchgoers. Three thousand souls is indeed a large parish. From what we read in the book of the Acts of the Apostles and elsewhere we can be certain that membership in the church in the apostolic age did not express itself by going to a large service once a week. The picture we have of the church in New Testament times is of a church that was cellular in structure. That is to say the membership in the larger body (the congregation) was built up from a commitment to the smaller unit of cells that met frequently (probably daily). Furthermore, those cells would not be specialization groups or groups convened around particular functions—prayer groups, discussion groups, or even Bible study groups. The cells would essentially be part of the larger body, but in each cell the ingredients of the larger church were always totally present and active: apostolic doctrine, fellowship, the breaking of bread, and prayer. In other words, the life of the whole would be fully present in the part in just the same way as the ingredients of the whole body are organically present in the one cell. The cell is not the same as a member of the body. It is the body in microcosm.

So with the church in apostolic times. For the larger experience of worship, the Christians (in the early days), would continue to go up to the temple.[16] Their distinctively Christian worship would almost certainly be in their houses. In other words, the church was not so much an organization and certainly not a building. It was more an organism and a whole way of life. It was life in the Spirit. In such groups, then and now, Christians experience God's power at work for salvation and healing in their midst. Christians enjoy the experience of Christ's authority and healing power through the faithful appropriation of the Scriptures, by receiving his word. There is a deep sense of fellowship and Christ is worshipped, adored, and obeyed as Lord of all. That fellowship is open and able to offer hospitality to those outside and, furthermore, it is able and very ready to move out and to serve the concerns of the local community and society around it. By actions as well as by words it is able to witness to Christ's power and God's grace, not only by exhorting people to go out and follow Jesus, but first by offering the Johanine injunction: "Come and see"—in a word, hospitality.

BAPTISM AND MINISTRY RESPONSIBILITY

Above all, baptism in the apostolic church is seen and experienced as ordination to ministry. We become Christians in order to be Christ for others. All baptism is for ministry. All the rich ministries listed in the New Testament provide a full orchestra of charisms and ministries, energized and employed in the church,

by the church, for the church, and so for the world. In that way
the body is built up; Jesus is glorified; the church is edified and
the kingdom furthered.

When this rich orchestra of ministries through baptism comes
alive, and when ministry is seen as a far larger word than the
ordained ministry, it is then that the ordained ministry of the
bishop and his local representative the presbyter (or priest) comes
into its own. For in the New Testament, there was a healthy
problem about and concern for unity. It was a healthy problem
that arose out of a lively church. The diversity and richness of
ministries within that church were so evident that order became
a necessary concern. There is always a need with such a large
and diverse orchestra of ministries as we find, for example, in the
Corinthian church to have overseeing, for the sake of unity and
order. However, this overseeing ministry is not there to have order
for its own sake and certainly not to quench the Spirit. Like a
good conductor, the ordained minister is never flamboyant or
overbearing! He respects the musicianship of the whole orchestra
far too much for him to become overtly demonstrative. The
healthy ordained ministry emerges out of a healthy and robust
orchestra of all the other ministries. Almost certainly, training
for the ordained ministry would be better undertaken in the
church today at least in its initial stages along with all the rest
of the ministries, in the school of the whole church, where the
saints are being equipped for ministry in the largest possible sense
of that word. It is only in that environment that the church can
best discern particular vocations that emerge as self-evident in
such a school of discipleship, teaching, and training. Seminaries
today need to be rooted in the larger baseline of training and
made available for the whole church. Only in this way shall we
keep training for the ordained ministry well and truly rooted in
the whole life of the whole body and in the setting of all the
other ministries that constitute the body of Christ.

It was Thomas Cranmer who in many ways caught the vision
of a non-clericalist church at the close of the Middle Ages. In
his prayer books he encouraged cells of the faithful to meet for
morning and evening prayer, to read the psalter and the Scriptures

and to say prayers as part of their daily Christian life. He did not intend those offices of morning and evening prayer to be muttered by the clergy in imitation of the medieval use of the Daily Office. There is strong evidence that he was powerfully motivated by Thomas More's vision of a commonwealth and a utopia and that for Cranmer the church was to be constituted under the Holy Spirit as bands and cells of men and women living the life of the spirit in a kind of spiritual commonwealth under the oversight of the ordained ministry of which the bishop was the model. The priest, rector, or curate was his local representative. Sadly this whole vision of corporate ministry, a corporate witness and the daily office has been lost over the centuries and largely ignored in the Anglican church precisely because in spite of all the reforms of the Reformation it is still largely a clericalist church. It was John Wesley with his strong doctrine of the church, who through cells, classes, and bands, sought to convene the church in the New Testament way, in the life of the Spirit. Renewal today, seems to have recaptured something of this vision in its new emphasis upon life in the spirit. In its turn it is bringing renewal in this way to the very roots of congregational life. In that sense renewal belongs to our tradition and is at last making evident what is locked within our tradition as Anglicans over the centuries. Furthermore, wherever the church comes alive in the life of the Spirit, it will be best ordered and re-ordered by a faithful preaching of the word and ministry of the Sacraments. In other words the ordained ministry need not feel threatened by the baptismal ministry! For where there is the emergence of a rich orchestra of ministries in the life of the local church, it is there that more rather than less will be demanded both from the local bishop and his local clergy. Simon Tugwell writes:

> It is to be hoped that we shall see a general revival in the church of all the various ministries and offices listed by St. Paul: for too long, the priest has had to shoulder the lot, and he is most unlikely to be naturally or supernaturally equipped for it. He needs the prophets and healers, and those gifted with supernatural wisdom and knowledge. If all those charismatic ministries are revived, this will probably consti-

tute more than anything else to the revival of the true charism of the priesthood, which will be freed of other burdens
to be itself.[17]

If that proves to be true of the ordained priesthood, it will prove
mutatis mutandis, to be even more true of the episcopate.

There can be no lasting renewal in the Episcopal church
without a renewal in our understanding of the episcopate. We
shall understand however the office of the episcopate best not
when we come to the matter from the point of view of the ordering
and organization of the ecclesiastical system. We shall discern the
office of the bishop best when we first contemplate the apostolic
nature of the mystery of the church. For it is in the climate of
witness, and even martyrdom, mission, and even evangelism that
we best perceive the apostolic nature of the church. For it is when
the church is being the church not for itself but for the world
that it is most faithful to the model of the apostolic church in
the early ages of Christianity and also most apparent as being
first and foremost the body of Christ. In all of this it is essentially
a band of men and women who are living the life of Christ in
the power of the Spirit. Such is the shape and nature of the inner
renewal of the church in every age; and conspicously in our own.

Notes

1. Acts 2:42.
2. Acts 2:41.
3. John 14:23.
4. Acts 4:32ff.
5. Acts 4:33a.
6. Acts 4:33b.
7. Isaac Watts, "When I survey the wondrous cross," *The Hymnal 1982*, No. 474.
8. 1 Corinthians 12:15.

9. 1 Corinthians 12:26.
10. 1 Corinthians 12:21.
11. Acts 2:47b.
12. William Barclay, *The Acts of the Apostles: The Daily Study Bible* (Place: The Saint Andrew Press, 1976), p. 30.
13. 1 Thessalonians 5:17.
14. Matthew 7:7.
15. See Luke 1:37.
16. See Acts 2:46.
17. Simon Tugwell, *Did You Receive the Spirit?* (London: Darton, Longman & Todd, 1972).

NINE

The Renewed Church
and the
Reformation of Society

THE GOSPEL AND SOCIETY

> It is exceedingly strange that any followers of Jesus Christ
> should ever have needed to ask whether social involvement
> was their concern and that controversy should have blown
> up over the relationship between evangelism and social re-
> sponsibility.[1]

Those opening words of John Stott constitute a summons at the
beginning of his book *Involvement* to all Christians, and especially
to evangelicals, to commit themselves, once again, to social action today as they did in earlier chapters of their renewal history.

It has to be freely admitted that critics of the renewal movement today do have a point when they accuse many of the leaders
most conspicuous in renewal of returning to their ecclesiastical
ghettos and of failing to carry out the mission of Christ beyond
the walls of their churches. Of course we can protest, and rightly,
that renewal both among evangelicals and catholics can cite some
remarkable chapters in their history, when social action and a
passion for justice and a care for the poor were all linked together

For much of the content of this chapter the author is indebted to the lecture
given at the Winter Park Conference by the Reverend Philip Turner.

in an attempt to reform and re-order society according to the laws of Christ. Nevertheless, it is interesting that in order to answer our critics we have to point to specific chapters and largely chapters that belong to our past history. It is frankly not so evident in our contemporary witness.

We may protest that too many liberals today have lost their direction and are up to their eyes in the debris of issues, conflicts, and political involvement. They have become so preoccupied with what has come to be called the social gospel that they have forgotten that there is a gospel at all. If they have any gospel left, it would seem that they have little motivation left to proclaim it, articulate it, preach it, or to evangelize—that is to say specifically to bring men and women to a personal knowledge of Jesus Christ as their Savior and Lord. At the present time, therefore, there is a spurious tendency to place evangelism over and against mission and to restrict the latter to the work of compassion and the call to care, which are both certainly inspired by the ministry and mission of Jesus Christ. All this has tended to put a cleavage between those who are most conspicuous in the name of mission and those who want to nail their colors to the mast of the Cross— the Cross of Jesus Christ, its summons and its priority in all evangelism. It has to be admitted further, that such passion as there is in mainstream churches today is most conspicuous in this area of social concern, justice, and the world order and not, as in former generations, in the areas of doctrine and spirituality. For example, the preacher in a seminary chapel denying the physical Resurrection of Jesus Christ would probably be met only with sophisticated silence. But the same preacher, in the same chapel, taking a stand (with either party) on abortion, for example, could well bring the service to a conclusion in nothing less than a riot and in outbursts of anger and disagreement.

Yet in all of this arena of division and sharp disagreement, we know (at our best and at our most renewed) that the renewal of the church must issue as surely in the reformation of society as that same renewal of the church in its turn issued straight out of the revelation of God. We simply cannot stop short at piety in place of spirituality. If renewal in the church is just a pietistic therapy for middle-class neuroses, then it is doomed to decay, to decline, and ultimately to be reduced to total irrelevance. If on the other hand, renewal is the reaffirmation of the lordship of Christ, as this book has suggested throughout, then we shall be obliged sooner rather than later to make sure that a renewed church witnesses to the breaking in of the kingdom—that kingdom in which Christ must rule over every aspect and corner of our lives and of our world. "In his hand are *all* the corners of the earth."[2] For as we have frequently testified: if Jesus is not Lord of all, he is not really Lord at all.

Furthermore, it has to be readily admitted that the mainstream churches need now and urgently to pick up the ticket of responsibility for the fragmentation of a liberal social concern that has apparently led many people to go outside the church to exercise care and compassion. For the same reasons as fundamentalism in our society is a judgment upon the mainstream churches, so it has to be said that liberal social concern, which is unrelated to the churches or to evangelism, is also a judgment upon us. After all in earlier chapters of the history of the church both among evangelicals and catholics, compassion and care for society as well as a willingness to tackle politically the issues and structures within that society have been remarkably conspicuous in the agendas of renewal.

THE RELATIONSHIP OF THE CHURCHES TO SOCIETY AT THE CLOSE OF THE TWENTIETH CENTURY

The first point we need to make, however, in discovering the link between the renewal of the church and the reformation of society is a point that at first appears to be more obviously historical and sociological than theological in the rather specific sense of that word. Put bluntly and drawn with a large sweep of the brush, we have to concede that the experiment of Constantine and its ensuing outworkings in the formation of church and society into a single unit called Christendom has come to an end. The enlightenment in Europe in the eighteenth century, after the religious wars of the Reformation, played havoc in a moral and ethical earthquake that brought the high-minded moral edifices of medieval theology tumbling to the ground. Furthermore, as the dust settled, it became apparent that the single and deep foundation on which high-rise morality and ethical conduct had been built for almost a thousand years could no longer be taken for granted. There was a shaking of the foundations. We were entering and are still in imprisoned in moral dark ages. Enlightenment virtues are built solely upon a temporal view of the universe, without God and where there are many contesting ideologies. In the enlightenment, it is the pursuit of happiness rather than the vision of God that is regarded as the ultimate goal of the human race.

Furthermore—and this is the really disturbing part—those enlightened virtues, like the horse of Troy, have entered within the very ramparts of the Christian church and have insinuated themselves so much into the life of Christians that the church can now only mirror back to society the false moral and ethical premises that society itself has produced. The church is failing to offer any challenge or any viable alternative. We have come out of Christendom in fact by the very opposite door from which we entered it. On entering Christendom we need to remember that the church in those days *gospelled* the secular society, challenging it, and ultimately changing it. On leaving Christendom, sadly, there is ample evidence to suggest that the very opposite has happened. The church today is challenged and changed by society rather than the other way round and the gospel is secularized to the point where it largely mirrors back only what it sees as self-evident in the world around it. An Episcopalian is, generally speaking, very much at home in the secular world. He leaves it to the Baptists or the extreme protestant sects to stick out like a sore thumb!

Second, this disengagement from the Constantinian unity of church and society means that our role as the Christian church has radically changed our relation to that society. The church is no longer the guardian and judge of public morality and although Christians do and indeed want from time to time to make their voice heard on various moral and political issues, that voice is on the whole increasingly marginalized. The church, if you like, is on the fringes and no longer where the action is, let alone called upon to referee the game. Psychologists and sociologists are more conspicuously wearing the uniform of referees than bishops or theologians today. And frankly, it is time that we recognized and acknowledged that there is no way back to a Constantinian view of the world and the church in Western society. In the West, we live in a post-Christian culture that does not even have the advantage of being a pagan culture. "A post-Christian man is not a pagan," C. S. Lewis sharply reminded us as long ago as 1954.

> It is a false idea that the historical process allows mere reversal; that Europe can come out of Christianity "by the same door as in she went" and find herself back where she was. It is not what happens. A post-Christian man is not a pagan: you might as well think that a married woman recovers her virginity by divorce.[3]

Church and society have in fact divorced and responsibility for the children's upbringing has been given by society to society and not to the church. We can no longer act as the moral policemen or referees of that society. We shall have to find another way of influencing society in the name of the gospel and frankly that is the challenge today to the renewed church. How do we do that? And what difference will it make to the church as well as to society if we seek to do this?

RECOVERING A STRATEGY FOR CHRISTIAN LIFE AND WITNESS

If the diagnosis of the situation as outlined above is in a broad sense true, it might explain why Christians are so sharply divided about social action both between their ranks and also within their ranks. There is the crunch for the church today.

> For the time has come for judgment to begin within the household of God; and if it begins with us, what will be the end of those who do not obey the gospel of God?[4]

The church as an institution infiltrating other institutions in society at every level as a kind of moral police force is no longer realistic. The Christian church today in the West is called upon once again to live its own common life (as in the Roman Empire when it was not an institution interwoven with all the other institutions of society). We are beginning to see (as was outlined in the last chapter) that the life of the Spirit in the common life of the body of Christ is all part of the gospel packaging. Common life belongs inextricably with the good news it seeks to proclaim. The general task of social responsibility is neither an isolated task for the church today nor can it be undertaken on the basis of individualism. Any idea that individuals can strike out with a prophetic message which has all the answers to society's ills is a delusion. The church itself has to embody and be a sign of its prophetic message. Acts 2:42 in particular constitute nothing less than a manifesto for the constitution of the church's own life. This does not mean that the church will form a ghetto in society. Ghetto formation is a mentality rather than a method. The church needs to be recalled to a radical re-grouping in order that it may first and foremost live the life which it longs to share with society. The problem begins when there is a credibility gap between the gospel that the church is proclaiming and the life that the church is living.

So we can see that the question has now moved in its emphasis. We now need to ask a different question. What moral and social issues must a *Christian* address if *we* (the church) are first to live in our society a common life which is in all essentials the life of the gospel? We do not have at our disposal broadcast statements on moral issues which we make, until we first discern what is disfiguring the body of Christ in its own common life. Philip Turner, in his presentation on this topic to the Winter Park Conference, suggested that first and foremost there are several primary issues that the church is called upon to put right within its own common life as the body of Christ, for Christians and among Christians. All of the issues that he raised were related to our care for the weak, blacks, the fetus, the terminally ill, the old, and the infirm. All those issues are not abstract causes, if they are first addressed within the body and the common life of that body. By Christian hospitality and by living in some sense in the extended family of the common life of the spirit, Christians need to begin to live together in such a way that they are both dealing with the issues and at the same time making a statement to society that challenges secularism and secular assumptions.

In other words, it needs to pursue an alternative life style. For the issues listed above are not abstractions. They are people and therefore more than mere problems. You can only solve problems with answers. People who have problems need to find a new way of living with those problems in a domestic hospitality that shelters them and sustains them until they grow beyond the problem. That is what the apostolic church did in its care for the widows and the poor. That is what Jesus means when he tells us that our primary task is to love one another.[5] It is interesting that he does not tell us that we must set out in one step to love the world outside. Judgment begins with the household of faith. The apostolic church lived the life while it was seeking to promulgate the message. In fact it had no message to give in abstraction apart from living the life. It refused to pander either to individualism on the one hand or moralism on the other. Both of these are evidently rife in much of our social witness today. Sadly, however, it is largely true to say that there is no visible or evident difference between the life style of Episcopalians today and the life of the society of which we are a part. Especially this is true in the realm of sexual ethics and the matter of material possessions. We simply mirror back to the secular world an ecclesiastical version of its own perversions. We are compromised before we open our mouths to address the issues by the very life style within our churches.

So the judgment must necessarily begin again (as in the apostolic age) with the household of faith. As Christians we are compelled to find urgently the answer to some of the issues listed above. The answers will not come about by administrative manifestos or slogans: it is only as we live the life, in the fellowship of the Spirit, that the answers will appear and will be self-authenticating. Much of our protest will be experienced by the simple invitation of Jesus: "Come and see." The life is being lived: problems are solutions in disguise. After all, Magellan discovered the world was round by sailing closer to the edge than anyone else before him! That is precisely where and how the Christian ship of the church needs to sail today—closer to the edges, where it can prove the power and truth of its gospel, challenging the prejudices and blindnesses of society, a society that is weary and largely spent.

This means that the Christian mind will be readily distinguished from the mind of the world, because like the mind of the world it will be fashioned and conditioned first by the society in which it is living—the common life of the body of Christ. Furthermore, we must not underestimate the witness and challenge that such a corporate life style can bring to the world. The word of God has power, real power, when it is united with the deed. The word is most articulate when it becomes flesh. So with the gospel message. When it is enfleshed in the common life of the church it sticks out like a sore thumb and by implication offers challenging alternatives to society. For that society (today as in the first century) is largely imprisoned within its own prejudices, which in their turn have been conditioned by the very environment of that society. There is huge evidence that wherever Christians have sought to tackle issues (especially those on their doorstep) by witnessing in public life and in practical local matters, they have and they do make an enormous difference.

Perhaps we do not acknowledge sufficiently that there is a real flight from public life and public responsibility in our world today in exactly the same way and probably for the same reasons as there was a flight from public life and responsibility in the days of the decline of the Roman Empire. The walls of secularism are not so secure or as resistant as they may appear. They may be more like the walls of Jericho than we imagine. In fact (again as in the case of the Roman Empire) when the fall comes it is swifter than we ever expected. "I looked and they were nowhere to be seen."[6] The Assyrian army withdrew in a night[7] and the Roman Empire fell within a single lifespan. At such times Christian leadership often finds itself summoned (as with Bishop Ambrose and many other Christian leaders in those days of decline) to take the reins of society. There is evidence of decay in the public

institutions of our large cities. Our society is in a crisis (in America and the West at least). We still enjoy enormous liberty, and
we should as Christians never tire of well-doing, certain in the
knowledge that society itself is crying out for renewal. Our culture
is seriously in decline. The spiritual ingredients that form a culture are sadly lacking in our own. This is even more a reason
why the church should be strategic in reconstruction and reformation. "Those that be with us are more than those that be with
them."[8]

THE PRIESTLY AND COMPASSIONATE COMMUNITY

The church is, at the end of the day, unlike any other institution
by its very nature. It was William Temple, the great Archbishop
of Canterbury, who used to remind Anglicans that the church
was the only society that existed for the sake of those who are
not members of it. That is what the priesthood of all believers is
all about. It is sad that the protestant Reformation of the sixteenth
century said so much about the priesthood of all believers and
did so little to implement its living reality in the life of the
church. In practice the Reformation did little more than to ex-
change one form of clericalism for another: The new presbyter
was but the old priest writ large. For, in fact, the doctrine of the
priesthood of all believers has nothing whatever to do with clericalism. It is a statement about the new life of the kingdom. In
evolution and nature until Jesus Christ it has been the law of the
jungle: every man for himself: the survival of the fittest, which
produced the law of competition throughout the whole of our
evolutionary history. But from Jesus Christ onward in these last
few seconds of time, which we call A.D., a new law has entered
the universe: it is man for others. It is the law of the new and
greater love of the kingdom: "Greater love hath no man than this
that a man lay down his life for his friends."[9] That is the greater
love—to live for others even to the point of death. Life for others:
that is the priestly life. It is not only a way of dying, but rather
it is a new way of living, and it has entered evolution just in the
nick of time, just in time to make all the difference between the

law of the jungle and the law of the kingdom: between ultimate self-annihilation for our universe as opposed to the possibility of new life in the kingdom. This quality of life is the hinge on which our universe, our evolution, and our destiny turns. The many are saved by the few as the few are saved by the one.

We can express it in another way. It is the life of intercession, which is not only a way of praying but rather a whole new way of living. In the Old Testament, Aaron, wearing the ephod with the arms of the twelve tribes of Israel over his heart, went into the Holy of Holies on behalf of all the tribes and not just his own. He entered on behalf of others into the presence of God. Aaron's tribe was the priestly tribe, the tribe of Levi. Our world needs at least one "tribe" in twelve to change the destiny and direction of history. Our world needs the leaven of this new and priestly way of living. The church is that priestly community. The ordained priesthood (in the person of the bishop primarily) is intended to minister in such a way as to make the church priestly. He does this by the preaching of the word and the ministration of the sacraments. In its turn, the church must become priestly in order that one day the kingdoms of this world, in which it is every man for himself, may become the kingdoms of our Christ and his God where it is every man for others. For in the kingdom you never have to pay for your own ticket. It has already been paid for by someone else. But the joke is that the minute you are in the kingdom you have to pay for the ticket for someone else. 'The unbelieving husband is sanctified by the believing wife and the unbelieving wife is sanctified by the believing husband."[10] Nothing less than this priestly character can be the goal for the Christian community.

In its turn the Christian community must produce and raise up leaders who will live as a sign both to the church and the world in this apostolic way. We call them bishops. Nevertheless, not all will be ordained in the church to this priestly ministry and perhaps the present large number of ordinands in the Epis-copal church is a sign that we have not fully articulated or under-stood clearly the high calling that is associated with our baptism. It is in our baptism that we enter into that quality of life, which is the call for us to be nothing less than Christ for others. That is the priestly life because it is essentially Christ's life; it is his way of living, which is almost certainly bound to issue in a way of dying. It is that death, which is itself a gateway to real life—life for others—the life of the kingdom. The most priestly activity we are ever called upon to perform by the institutional church as laity is the responsibility of being a god-parent. We pledge our faith on behalf of others; that is a very priestly calling indeed. But it needs to represent symbolically the whole relationship of the church to society as it represents specifically the relationship of Jesus Christ the one great high priest to the rest of the priestly community, the body of the redeemed, the church.

We live that priestly life, however, as the priesthood of all believers, which is certainly not the same as the priesthood of every believer. Our corporate life in the spirit, if it is lived in this way, can never degenerate and must never degenerate into a ghetto mentality. The church will become a kind of hospice in its hospitality for all those who are *in extremis.* It will not mean that we have all the answers to the ills of society. But rather, living the apostolic life of dislocation we will be in the place where God wants us to be, in the place where society needs us to be and living in a manner and style of life that the gospel demands us to do. For apostolic life is dislocated life, as surely as Jesus was dislocated from the life of the Trinity to extend to us the hospitality of the divine Godhead. Christ is the model of apostle in the same way that he is the model of priesthood. Christians, therefore, are aliens in a foreign land; living together the life, because there is no other way of living that life except together. Only such corporate life can bring to the ills of this world in the place and in the manner needed, the compassion of Christ. While we must never underestimate what can be achieved to change the structures of society by responsible involvement, there must always be the overriding willingness to enter the battle even if we do not have all the answers for a successful victory.

Holding the dying leper in his arms, with no easy answers to the problem that permit such deprivation, and seemingly with no power at our disposal to change the principalities and powers of a society that actually promotes such a sickness, we can and must still say and go on saying, many times: "Dear brother, Jesus loves you." We know that such words are no substitute for changing the structures of our society, but in their turn even changed structures will not exonerate us from the compulsion to say and to go on saying, in season and out of season, when we have the answers and when we do not have the answers: "Dear brother, Jesus loves you." At that point (enfolded in the arms of love and priestly compassion) evangelism and mission are but two sides of the same gospel coinage. In other words, we are, as the priestly community, living the apostolic life related to the social issues of our world because God is related to the issues of our world through the incarnation of Christ. And furthermore, we do not have to wait to do all this until we have the answers to solve all the problems. Christ died his priestly death while we were yet sinners and sinning. He did not wait to change the world or to have all the answers. His priestly body, the church, must live that priestly death, while the world is still under the power of Satan, and neither flee from the responsibility of trying to change the world, nor wait for the world first to change, nor even wait until we have all the perfect answers.

In the meantime the Christian will live out the Christian life in the corporate life of the Spirit, the body of Christ, the church. That church itself will be a kind of laboratory in which we test and prove the truth of the gospel message. It will be the basis of our credibility. It will be the storehouse of the riches of the kingdom. It is as we live that life and alongside that life that we shall meet the issues of the world with compassion, with conviction, and with confidence. Our confidence, however, will be in Christ—Christ, God's way of being human. But it will be as we live the life that we discover the answers. The answers will not be for export only. They must be lived in the context of prayer, worship, preaching, the sacraments, and, above all, the fellowship of the Spirit.

The apostolic life in which the whole church participates is a crucial sign to our world. That sign has to be lived before it can be exported. There can be no reformation of society in the name of the gospel until the church is renewed and is living that gospel. Those are hard and challenging words to say to the church today. Unless we hear them and receive them gladly, all our talk will be but vain words full of sound and fury, yet signifying absolutely nothing.

Notes

1. John Stott, *Involvement* (Place, N.J.: Fleming H. Revell Co., 1984), 1:19.
2. Psalms 95:4.
3. C. S. Lewis, "De Descriptione Temporum," in *They Asked for a Paper* (London: Geoffrey Bles, 1962), p. 20.
4. 1 Peter 4:17.
5. John 13:35.
6. Psalms
7. See 2 Kings 19:35.
8. 2 Kings 6:16.
9. John 15:13.
10. 1 Corinthians 7:14.

EPILOGUE

An Unfinished Agenda

I had hoped to keep the writing of this book out of the first person. As I come to the conclusion, however, I fear it is impossible to do so. The book was occasioned by a conference. I was invited to write this book before the conference began by the convening committee. As I have said elsewhere, this is neither a report of that conference nor is it right to assume that what is written in this book would commend itself necessarily in every detail to everyone who attended that conference. At best, what has been written in these pages comes straight out of the spirit of that conference. In fact, I wrote the book in eight days immediately following the conference.

Yet as I have written this, something else has become clear to me. There is a strain of autobiography in this book that has lent something of a compulsive element both to the style and content of what is found in these pages. In a word, I had to write this book. There were moments when it seemed as though the book was writing itself for me.

For in truth, so much of what I have written springs from a deep commitment to the Anglican church worldwide and to the Episcopal church in particular. After nearly twenty-four years in Orders, I left South London (England), where I had been a bishop for just over nine years, to begin the Anglican Institute. The

Anglican Institute was founded on a vision, a vision that Anglicanism was and is truly part of God's divine plan for his whole catholic church. The Anglican Institute is a missionary society, founded in St. Louis, to be a powerful mission to our church—to recall the Anglican church internationally and the Episcopal church here in the States to its own powerfully gospel-shaped credentials. I am an Anglican by conviction and not by convenience. By birth and upbringing I was a Roman Catholic. By temperament I would probably choose to be Russian Orthodox for its music, its liturgy, its history, and its spirituality. But by conviction and by the scruff of the neck I am a passionate Anglican.

I am deeply saddened, therefore, by what I see happening in the Church of England, and many will say after reading this book, with something of a note of aggression in their voice—"Go home and prophesy there!" The Church of England in the 1980s is sadly dwindling in size and influence. The numbers of committed communicants were down yet again in 1985 to 1.2 million—an all-time low. The Roman Catholic church in England is now the largest church numerically and in spite of many problems continues to grow. But I am not seeking here to make a denominational point, please let that be clear. Wherever and however Jesus is glorified in his church—that is and must always be the geography of our first love and our first commitment irrespective of denominational labels.

It is the stubbornness and the refusal of the Church of England to reach out and learn now from outside of its own limited traditions, it is that which pains most. There is a refusal to look either to the black church in Africa, which is white-hot with gospel witness, or to turn to the Episcopal church in the States, where there is a robust vitality and a sense of life and aggressive mission. It is this doctrinaire retrenchment of liberalism in all its forms in the Church of England that is blinding that church to any movement to renew it effectively. It is the Anglican Communion worldwide outside the Church of England where hope lies for renewal in the Mother church, if only there is humility and readiness to learn lessons from our fellowship of churches in the rest of the world (not least the Third World) and not least

also from across the waters from the Episcopal church where the
renewal movements are so evidently at work.

All is not well in the Episcopal church: far from it. Yet, the
frontier mentality and the faith of Abraham to strike out are not
so entirely dissimilar. Renewal, along the lines outlined in this
book is happening. God is renewing his church. The Episcopal
church, relatively small though it is, nevertheless is growing again
both in numbers and influence. Catholic, scriptural, thinking
Christianity can be discerned among its ranks and could well
form a vital and crucial convergence that can speak to American
religion at a turning point in America's history. Perhaps it takes
an English episcopal exile to recognize this perspective and to
articulate it with passion. For the convergence of the saints is
here, and it is here for a purpose. There is real evidence that
where the full ingredients of a gospel, catholic, Spirit-filled and
thinking church are found, many come to know the Lord. Lives
are changed. The fruits of the Spirit are evident. There are new
Christians and Christians are made new. The local community
beyond the walls of the church is powerfully affected, lifted, and
radically refashioned by the presence and powerful ministry and
witness of such a church. *In a word it still works.*

One of the most telling points in the Winter Park Conference
was an evening program where we heard the record of four very
different priests and pastors about renewal at grassroots level in
their parishes. As the open letter to the churches makes evident,
printed elsewhere in this book, the four pastors are from differing
traditions and churchmanships within Anglicanism and are located in four very different social settings. As the four pastors
told their stories (wonderfully free from any mark of triumphalism), it became evident that there were, alongside all the differences between their stories, striking constants. We need to note
these constants very carefully. They tell us a great deal about the
shape and content of renewal from the point of view of those
whose responsibility it is to minister the Word and Sacraments.

The first and most evident feature common to renewed parish
ministry is the centrality and primacy of Jesus as the Lord of his
church, Lord of Scripture, and Lord of history. At one level you

might say that this should hardly need to be said. Nevertheless, it does have to be said. Jesus first and Jesus last—whether in the Mass or in the preaching of the word. Furthermore, it is Jesus as traditionally worshipped, adored, and obeyed—Jesus in the flesh, the Jesus of history, and the Christ of the cosmos. Jesus for these four pastors was no mere idea or proposition. Jesus was their Lord and his Lordship spread throughout their congregations and those for whom they were pastorally responsible. But above all, it was Jesus as the source of all strength and power that was so evident in all of their ministries. There was a radical, almost incandescent, New Testament dependence upon him upon whom all else depends. Christianity is Jesus Christ, yesterday, today, and for ever.

All four pastors had experience of renewal in their parish pastorates, because they had stayed there. "Stay in the city until you are clothed with power from on high."[1] These four witnesses refused to talk in "career" terms. All moves from their point of view in the church are horizontal. Sadly there is a tendency today for clergy to use their congregations as steps on a career ladder. The laity recognize this very quickly and feel all too easily walked on and passed over. We should be thinking in terms today (as in earlier ages) of ten to fifteen years as the normal span of ministry in one place rather than five to ten years as it is at the present. Every additional year after the first five, where there is renewal in the life of the priest and his people, represents compound rather than simple interest. The pastor in these situations sees his or her call as part of the total calling by God to the whole parish. The priest is not in a separate category pursuing his clerical calling. God's call to commitment is to all his people. They are in it together.

All four of those who gave evidence on that memorable evening at the Winter Park conference exercised strong leadership styles—this by God's grace, with all due humility, yet refusing to lay aside real responsibility as leaders.

But this commitment both for clergy and laity in the cells of Christian life in their parishes went very deep. It went deep enough to go to the point of suffering itself. In areas of deprivation, unemployment, economic recession, or just the disintegration and fragmentation that characterize huge areas of city life today, the church enters with compassion into the suffering of humanity. Jesus continues to bear in his body those very scars that are most strikingly evident by contrast wherever resurrection witness is being exercised. So if "one member suffers, all suffer together, if one member is honored all rejoice together."[2]

Yet even in areas with all the problems of urban disintegration, the Christian presence is called upon to witness not so much to problems but rather to promises: Christ's promises. In other words, there must be evangelism in many forms. One particular form is in the ministry of healing. There is no room for moralism in these kind of parishes (there is no room for moralism anywhere on the earth) but there is a deep need for reconciliation, forgiveness, and healing, and for the Christian community to be a sign of that work of Christ in its preaching, in the Sacraments, and in the fellowship of the Spirit.

Worship in all four parishes and in four very different traditions has a high priority indeed. Worship is never to be trivialized or underestimated in importance in all pastoral situations. The church is most visibly the church in its worship if that worship is *gospelled* by the Word. Furthermore, the worship must be well thought out and printed out in such a way that it is easy of access for all newcomers. There must be an expectation that there will indeed always be newcomers and strangers in our midst. They are the very people that we are in business for. And every service or gathering of the church must expect to be richly blessed and graced by the presence of God. God is at work mightily among His people. It is still happening. It still works. "It is the Lord's doing and it is marvelous in our eyes."

At the end of that evening, I went back to my hotel bedroom, recalling nine years as a bishop and feeling that most of that time had been spent on matters of only secondary importance. The reorganization of parish and even diocesan boundaries had taken up massive amounts of time, money, manpower, and of course paper. I am not saying that some of this was not important business for the church, but frankly after hearing the evidence from

these four pastors, I felt as though so much of the pastoral oversight I had exercised as a bishop in a diocese was really so much
re-organization of the furniture on the deck of the ecclesiastical
Titanic. What the church needs is to go out and find more and
more men and women and train them in such a way that they in
their turn will go out and do the job more or less in the same
way as pastors and preachers and priests have done it ever since
the church began. There is nothing new about real renewal. Of
course, the four pastors on that evening were not soloists. They
would be the first to witness to a genuine team ministry with all
the laity in their parishes. They saw the task of the pastorate as
a corporate task involving all the ministries of the New Testament
and not just simply the ordained ministry of Word and Sacrament.
Nevertheless, it has to be admitted that the head of the body
(sacramentally) is the priest or pastor of the congregation. If there
is not renewal in the head, it is difficult for there to be renewal
that is not divisive among all the members. We need to pray for
and to work for the renewal of the clergy.

SO WHAT ABOUT THE SEMINARIES?

This brings me to three cries from the heart, largely unarticulated
as such at the Winter Park Conference, but always significantly
just below the surface of our deliberations. What are we to do
about our seminaries? Are they doing the job they are there to
do? Are they turning out ministers of Word and Sacrament who
are renewed and refreshed by the Spirit with Justin Martyr's
"flame in the mind" and on fire in their hearts with the love of
Jesus Christ? Or are we rather turning out people for whom Christianity is largely an idea, perpetually open to discussion; an ideology inviting a program for the improvement of society; for whom
a sermon is primarily an essay and for whom worship is another
service that has to be conducted? Do seminaries substitute counseling for Christian formation and produce managers in place of
prophets? I think the answer has to be said that on the whole
they do. Furthermore, do we need to see a radically new place
for seminaries in the total life of the whole church? Should they

be primarily clergy factories or should they be centers of renewal for the training and equipping of the *whole* people of God for ministry and mission? Of course, in that bigger strategy the particular call to the ordained ministry would have its special (yet limited) place. The whole idea of a seminary was largely the invention in the first place of a clericalist church for a clericalist ministry. The renewal movement today has moved our understanding both of the nature of the church and the richness and diversity of the ministry far beyond largely nineteenth-century and Roman Catholic understandings. The location of our seminaries in relation to the rest of the life of the church and their programs needs today a radical shift, if they are to serve the whole church for mission and not merely for maintenance.

BISHOPS, YES, BUT WHAT SORT?

There can be no lasting renewal in an Episcopal church that is not divisive or sectarian without a renewal in our understanding of the Episcopal office. We need more bishops, fewer priests, more deacons, and above all more Christians who are graced, trained, and equipped to spend less time at church meetings and more time as a lay apostolate in and for the world. In a renewed and reshaped church, the bishop will have less glory and tinsel and more power and punch. We need less prelacy and better episcopacy among our bishops; less clericalism and more ministry among our clergy; less churchiness and more witness among our laity. The key that will unlock such a church to be truly apostolic in this way will be a true apostle in our midst. Bishops need to live and minister on the frontiers of faith where the new Christians are won. Karl Rahner writes:

> The possibility of winning new Christians from a milieu which has become unchristian is the sole living and convincing evidence that even today Christianity still has a real chance for the future. . . . It means more to win one new Christian from what we may call neopaganism than to keep ten "old Christians."[3]

So Rahner deduces in a telling passage:

> If . . . we want to choose a bishop . . . we ought not to ask
> so much whether the candidate has adapted himself very
> smoothly to the traditional machinery of the church or
> whether he has done well what people expected of him in
> the light of the traditional behaviour patterns of office holders
> in the church. We ought to ask rather if he has ever suc-
> ceeded in getting a hearing from the "neopagans" and made
> at least one or two of these into Christians. [4]

What about that on the profile for the search committee? A man
of mission, please, not of maintenance. An evangelist, an apologist, and a teacher, and preacher. Those are the ingredients of
the apostolic life. For here is the warning. Unless the bishops are
conspicuous in these ministries and on the frontiers of renewal,
with discernment, leadership, and living with the community of
the church in the life of the Spirit, located within renewal, then
it does not mean that renewal will cease. Renewal is here to stay.
It does mean, however, that such renewal that takes place outside
of the Episcopal structures of the church will, as it so often has
in the past, become divisive and sectarian. Renewal needs the
bishops, but, goodness knows, the bishops are in need of renewal.

DECISION MAKING

Third, if we are not to hinder and frustrate the growing appeal
and sign of renewal in the Episcopal church, we have simply got
to stop tearing ourselves apart by lurching from one issue to another and one crisis to another in the continuing saga of General
Conventions. In other words, we shall have to discover an appropriate way of decision making in our church that is neither divisive nor hysterical. At least, thank goodness, in the Episcopal
church, General Convention meets only once every three years.
In the Church of England, where they seem to have got the synod
on the brain, the General Synod actually meets three times each
year! There is a whole bureaucracy set up within the Church of
England to keep such a synod program going with suitably long

agendas and to maintain and build up all the mountains of paper associated with it.

But for our whole church today, in Anglicanism decision making is important because we need to get it right. There are no easy answers. What is apparent, however, is that an ecclesiastical version of parliaments and congresses working to achieve majorities and convening in party groups is neither the way the New Testament church conducted its business, nor is it the way for a gospel church today to do its homework. Many parishes have gone over to the method of consensus and unanimity in conducting their local life rather than the way of majorities where there are winners and losers. In his book *Decision Making in the Church: A Biblical Model,* Professor Luke Johnson suggests a more biblical model for decision making. This is an urgent and important debate we sorely need in our church today: how are we to make decisions? After all, the biblical model that is outlined in that book brought the church through the first and perhaps the greatest of all of its crises in decision making, the whole Gentile issue. If it served the church in the name of unity, truth, and love, then perhaps it has something to say to us with our comparatively trivial issues today.

THE SHAPE OF THE CHURCH TO COME: A DREAM

The convergence of the saints is with us. We need to recognize it, celebrate it, and invite all to join with us on the road of renewal, unity, and mission. But renewal must not become another new party in the church: a question of those who are and those who are not. Our gaze will not be focused in that self-conscious way upon ourselves, but rather upon Him, who always makes us feel just a little unsettled by that feeling that however far we have traveled and however late in the day it is, he still makes as though he would go further. For there must be no settling down and building booths, let alone mansions. The call has gone out, and once again we are aware that we are an exodus people, continually called out from our entrenched positions to a place of meeting and to a point beyond where we have ever been before.

Yet in a sense we know that we have been this way many times
before, though now it would seem that we know it perhaps for
the first time. The renewed church, where the saints are converging is a richer church than we thought could ever be possible.

> The way forward to this pleroma and richness . . . is for each
> Christian community to arrive at the point of convergence
> and persistently speak only of those things which they wish
> to affirm, remaining silent about those things which they are
> against. Thus the agenda at the point of convergence would
> be the re-affirmation of many insights which in the past have
> divided us. Some would be for an all-member ministry; oth-
> ers would be for various charismatic ministries; others would
> be for a stronger and more robust doctrine of the Bible; others
> would wish to set the place of lively liturgy high on the
> agenda. All of these would be affirmations. There would be
> no place to hear what we are against! So much of what we
> have been against has been clothed in the accidents of his-
> tory. Much opposition to episcopacy has rightly been because
> that episcopacy in many ages was seen as prelacy. Much op-
> position to priesthood and the other ordained ministries has
> justifiably arisen because in the past it has been a package
> deal with clericalism. Renewal has moved the argument along
> and we need to follow it and to make sure that we are not
> simply rehearsing divisions of the past or the reasoning of
> the past. Hopefully, we shall find that many of these affir-
> mations are not so exclusive or divisive as they appeared to
> be in their original historical setting.[5]

Such is the challenge that renewal extends today. Such was
the challenge we experienced at the Winter Park Conference.
Jesus Christ is being raised up again by His Father as Lord of his
church, Lord of the Scriptures, and Lord of history. We must not
settle for continually recounting only the bad news because we
have set our eyes upon it and remained standing still, looking sad
and talking only of the disasters, the mistakes, and pains of the
past in our common life. God in Christ has met us on the road
at our point of need and of our greatest impotence, just as he met
those two disciples on the road to Emmaus. The question is the

same to us as it was to those two disciples. Do we know him and can we recognize this Jesus in our midst? Always at any time of the day or night, he is still that same Jesus who opens the Scriptures and tells us the things concerning himself, if we will let him. He is that Jesus who is present at the breaking of the bread and in the fellowship of wherever two or three are gathered together in his name.

But still, he makes as though he would go further. For the agenda is unfinished, and time itself will not end until there is time to finish this agenda. It is his agenda and mighty acts, with new glories still to reveal and new opportunities for even greater grace to be given. For wherever disciples encounter their risen Lord he gives them an abundance of his grace to turn them around and the strength to go back to face the conflict in the city, in the company of the church, and in the fellowship of the Spirit. Yet, he still makes as though he would go further and the agenda is still unfinished.

For, always, in another sense, the agenda is the same. "The Lord is risen, the Lord is risen indeed" they keep saying in different languages and in new tongues. So this same Jesus continues to make himself known to his disciples on the road of their discipleship turning disciples into apostles and sinners into saints. And again and again, every split second now, unending day and night, while, when, and wherever this is happening, and at the same moment of need this same Jesus is breaking through the doors of our divisions and our fears and making Himself known to us in our midst.

And so it goes on. And so it will continue to go on, as it was in the beginning is now and shall be for ever. World without end. Amen.

Notes

1. Luke 24:49b.
2. 1 Corinthians 12:26b.

3. Karl Rahner, *The Shape of the Church to Come* (London: SPCK, 1972), p. 33.
4. Ibid.
5. Michael Marshall, *The Anglican Church: Today and Tomorrow* (Wilton, Conn.: Morehouse Barlow, 1984), p. 142.

Appendices

APPENDIX I

Revelation, Renewal, and Reformation
A Statement of United Purpose
Winter Park, Florida; 10 January 1986

We are bishops, priests, and laity from the three streams of renewal in the Episcopal church—catholic, evangelical, and charismatic. At a conference January 7–10, we met to seek the Lord's
guidance for renewal in the Episcopal church. We recognized a
spirit of unity and a great work God is accomplishing in our
church: the convergence of the three streams as a sign to our
times. Our common knowledge of Christ and our love for him
and for our brothers and sisters also trying to serve him compel
us to share with the whole church what we have seen and heard.

Theological presentations by Anglican leaders undergirded the
conference. Parish priests told of renewal in their congregations
and communities. All ninety participants joined in group discussions of issues vital to renewal: authority, salvation, preaching,
apostolic witness, life in the Spirit, and evangelism and mission.

THEOLOGICAL RENEWAL

Four speakers gave us a theological basis on which to do our work.
In his keynote address, the Rev. Dr. J.I. Packer, professor of sys-
tematic theology at Regent College, defined our points of agreement and called for unity. The Reverend Peter Moore, chairman
of the board of Trinity Episcopal School for Ministry, asserted the

authority of Scripture. Bishop Michael Marshall, Episcopal director of the Anglican Institute, presented the church as a sign of the gospel. The Reverend Dr. Philip Turner, professor of Christian ethics at General Seminary, set forth the spiritual mandate for the renewed church's public witness. These theological analyses moved us beyond barriers of partisanship and prejudice and into the constructive work of the conference.

PARISH RENEWAL

Four rectors set before us the present reality of renewal in parishes where Christ is building his church.

Father Keith Ackerman is rector of St. Mary's in Charleroi, Pennsylvania, an Anglo-Catholic parish where people are out of work and were out of hope. As he has shared Jesus with his community, the congregation has more than doubled. More important, a new spirit of joy and hope has replaced the sense of despair.

From a base at St. Stephen's Church in Sewickley, the Reverend John Guest's extraordinary ministry of evangelism has challenged the city of Pittsburgh for Jesus Christ. In the process, his parish has grown phenomenally in numbers, witness, and service.

The comprehensive biblical teaching of the Reverend John Howe, rector of Truro Church, Fairfax, Virginia, has led this congregation into extensive charismatic renewal. For four years the congregation has given 50% of the annual parish budget to outreach.

The Reverend Carol Anderson, rector of All Angels Church in New York City, has found ministry to the poor and dispossessed to be a central expression of renewal in her parish. Her growing congregation includes a diverse mix of street people, young professionals, and artists. Accepting people as they are, the congregation of All Angels sees lives transformed by the power of the Holy Spirit.

These four leaders, from different traditions and in different circumstances, have this in common: all confess the centrality of Jesus in their ministry; all have been led by an extravagant vision of hope for their congregations and communities; and yet all have had to sacrifice and persevere for the sake of the Lord's work. These witnesses certify the renewing activity of the Holy Spirit in our church.

REFLECTIONS ON RENEWAL

In six working groups, we explored dimensions of renewal and discovered the rich extent of our agreement on the basics of the faith. We believe the Lord has spoken to us in these areas:

Authority. Our experience of renewal has confirmed the classic Anglican understanding of theology as built upon Scripture, reason, and tradition, in that order of priority, as Richard Hooker plainly taught. Scripture is "God's Word written," and we know it provides the basis for our discernment of truth, food for our nurture, light upon our path, correction to our way, and instruction in holy living. We believe the Scriptures are completely trustworthy and sufficient for salvation, so that in all things God's will may be accomplished in praise of Jesus, his Son. This has been the authority for Christian life and practice since early days. We commit ourselves to honor once again the priority of Scripture, that we in the church may again enjoy the blessing it promises.

Salvation. The act of God which sets us free from the power of evil, sin, and death began when God graciously reached out to restore his creation to himself. We affirm that in his suffering and death, Jesus offered himself as a sacrifice for us. His actual resurrection from the dead attested his divinity, vindicated his claims, and broke the power of sin and death once for all.

It is only by his grace that we are able to respond to this gift. Through repentance, faith, and conversion of life, we appropriate his promises. By his Spirit we are reborn, justified, and sanctified. In the worshiping and believing community, we celebrate Jesus' passion, death, resurrection, and ascension. In the Rites of Initiation, we die and rise with Christ. In the Eucharist, we are fed, have a foretaste of heaven, remember his death, and celebrate his risen life until he comes again.

Preaching.   Preaching has authority when it takes us to the God of the Bible. It has the power to convey salvation by establishing a connection between God's love, judgment, and mercy and the minds and hearts of a congregation. The preacher must have experienced this life-changing power, must be a biblical person submitted to Jesus Christ as he is revealed in the Scriptures, and must be convinced of the urgency and authority of this task.

Apostolic Witness.   We of the ordained ministry, recognizing previous failures, are committing ourselves afresh to learn from God in the Scriptures, abstain from conformity to the world, and come under the lordship of Jesus. We believe people must be challenged to surrender and commit their lives to Jesus as Lord and Savior and thereby begin to grow to spiritual maturity. We desire to return to the basics of the apostolic faith—preaching, teaching, breaking of the bread of eucharist, prayer, and holiness of life. We stand in fear and trembling, knowing that to this our Lord has called us, and for this he holds us accountable.

Life in the Spirit.   Episcopal churches rarely expect or experience God's power and the fellowship that the Holy Spirit makes available. We are convinced that the church will not experience this power and fellowship until it gives a scriptural answer to the question, What think ye of Christ?

We testify that the scriptural promises of supernatural resources to the believer are true. We have experienced the Spirit's work in the lives of individuals and the church. We believe that God desires all his people to be empowered witnesses to Christ and effective channels of his gifts and grace. Our witness is that the personal experience of the Holy Spirit quickens worship in the church. It becomes alive and vibrant, confirming faith and encouraging witness.

Evangelism and Mission.   Evangelism is the presentation of

Jesus Christ in the power of the Holy Spirit. People are called to personal commitment through repentance and faith, confessing the lordship of Christ within the fellowship of the church. Therefore, we are called to proclaim the only hope for the world.

Yet personal evangelism without commitment to global mission lacks the authentic integrity of the gospel. Submitted to the Spirit, we must honor the Word of God, which proclaims the gospel as good news to the poor. We are Christ's eyes and ears to discern the needs of those he loves—our neighbor across the street or across the sea. We are his hands and feet to go and serve in his name.

We are convinced that in following Christ we have no choice but to become involved in issues of our day. The kingdom must be proclaimed! But our lead must come from God rather than from the world, from his Word that teaches his way of justice and compassion. We know that when the Spirit renews the lives of individuals or congregations, that renewal will die unless they continue to move beyond themselves. The Spirit challenges those whom he renews to change practices and policies that compromise his witness to full expression of God's righteous love, both in church and in society, globally and locally.

THE FUTURE OF RENEWAL

We recognize that the Spirit is moving in our midst, and our purpose is to move with him. Like the apostles, "we cannot but speak of what we have seen and heard" (Acts 4:20). Our experience of the presence and power of our Lord in this conference has led us to resolve to work together, not separately, toward renewal within the Episcopal church. We invite all Episcopalians to join us in our quest for spiritual renewal through the Holy Spirit.

Where Jesus Christ is known, trusted, loved, and adored; where the sinner is loved but all forms of sin are hated and renounced; where Christ's living presence is sought and found in fellowship; and where righteousness is done—there the church is in renewal, in whatever variety of worship and devotion the new life finds expression.

> If you have any encouragement from being united with Christ, if any comfort from his love, if any fellowship with the Spirit, if any tenderness and compassion, then make my joy complete by being like-minded, having the same love, being one in spirit and purpose.   (Philippians 2:1–2)

APPENDIX II

"*Our Testimony Today*"

A statement inspired by the Conference at Winter Park, Florida, and written by the Rev. J.I. Packer and by Bishop Michael Marshall, representing two opposite but by no means opposing ends in the spectrum of renewal in our church today.

When the Lord restored the fortunes of Zion,
we were like those who dream.
Then our mouth was filled with laughter,
and our tongue with shouts of joy;
then they said among the nations,
"The Lord has done great things for them."
The Lord has done great things for us;
we are glad.   (Psalm 126:1–3)

This is our testimony today.

Who are we? We are a company of clergy and laity representing the three streams of renewal that have emerged in the Episcopal Church during the past quarter of a century: catholic; evangelical and charismatic. We met by invitation in Orlando, Florida, for the "Three Rs" Conference, to explore together the themes of the Revelation of God, the Renewal of the Church and the Reformation of Society, and to seek together a cohesive renewal strategy to guide the Episcopal Church for fifteen years, to the end of this century. The Lord has been with us, and now we offer this Statement to the Church so that we may fully share what we have been vividly shown.

Conference presentations have made clear to us the meaning

of renewal with a breadth, depth, and unitive force that has brought wonder and joy to us all. We have discerned the God-given "convergence of the saints" in appreciating the New Covenant ministry of the Holy Spirit. This is a momentous new development in our time, and one of which Christ through the Spirit has graciously made us part. Theological analysis has verified our hope that a deeper understanding and experience of the Spirit's ministry would enable us to transcend inherited barriers of party position and party spirit. We see our convergence which we have found to be so fruitful, as still continuing, drawing us on to greater riches in the Spirit than any of us have yet known. It is out of the common knowledge of Christ and the shared love for Him and for each other in Him to which the Spirit has brought us, that our Statement flows.

The Spirit Himself has renewed our confidence in the trinitarian, incarnational, redemptive faith of the Bible and the Creeds, the faith that focuses on the saving and transforming power of our crucified, risen, reigning, and returning Lord.

The Spirit has given us new confidence in the Bible. The Bible is the embodiment and instrument of revelation, which the Spirit Himself inspired and which he now authenticates and interprets in the fellowship of the faithful. We prize the Scriptures as our divine rule and guide for the whole of our faith, life, and service, and our divine resource for every form of worship, proclamation, and pastoral care.

The Spirit has also renewed our vision of the church as the theatre of power and glory in which Jesus Christ, our exalted Head, is being formed in his members by his own unbelievable grace through the ministry of word and sacrament and the life of worship and fellowship. The Savior whom we honor is one who by his Spirit is re-creating in himself the broken earthenware of fallen humanity, both ours and that of our fellow believers with whom we share Christ's forgiveness and the give-and-take of family fellowship in the local congregation. We have been shown afresh that it is through us, as limbs in his body, that this great Savior reaches out in compassionate evangelism and Samaritanship to serve human needs. We have rededicated ourselves to this our Christian and churchly calling, with all the joys and pains that it will bring.

As for renewal, the Spirit has shown us that where, in accordance with the Scriptures, Jesus Christ is known, trusted, loved and adored as Savior, Master, and Friend; where all forms of sin are hated and renounced; where Christ's living presence is sought and found in the fellowship of his people; and where action is ruled by the passion to do righteousness, to make others great before God, and thus to glorify our glorious Lord; there the church is in renewal, in whatever variety of liturgical and devotional forms the new life finds expression. It is obedience to the lordship of Christ that gives authority to the preaching of the gospel and the witness of the church. Renewal begins as obedience is recovered.

We know, and would insist, that the church becomes credible as a sign of the reality of Christ and his grace as it is ever more deeply conformed to the likeness of Jesus in his death and resurrection. We are clear that only a church that is converted and controlled by the word of God, in which the mind of Christ is formed in truth and love by the Holy Spirit, is equipped to reform community structures according to the pattern of the kingdom of God as the gospel reveals it to us. Compassion without conversion offers only ineffective palliatives for human pain and social ills.

Our experience of the presence and power of our Lord in this conference, showing us his truth and pouring out upon us his Spirit within our converging frames of renewal, has led us to resolve that for the future we will pursue renewal within the Episcopal Church, not separately, but together. We shall seek to recover everywhere the realities of love for Christ our Savior, and a simple, childlike obedience to his commands, with which renewal begins.

Nor did the Holy Spirit stop short at unifying our thoughts and goals with regard to renewal, momentous milestone as that oneness of mind and heart truly is. The Spirit went on to set before us the present reality of renewal in different parishes in which Christ is wonderfully building his church, ranging from the frenetic inner city to a working-class wilderness of unemployment to affluent, complacent suburbia to the world of sophisticated pragmatists and power-brokers. The Spirit alerted us afresh to the need for "every-member ministry" to be the rule in the renewed body of Christ and to the equal importance of the service of gifted layfolk with that of the clergy. We came to see the special strength of the symbiotic relationship whereby all local ministry, clerical and lay, is related to the Bishop and through the Bishop to wider experiences of renewal throughout the dioceses. An Episcopacy that is committed to serving renewal in the church in this way will constantly facilitate the flow of renewal from individual parishes into the wider fellowship of the world-wide people of God. We find that our commitment to the Episcopal church system is not weakened, but strengthened by our own experiences of renewal, as we recognize the spiritual dynamics and potential of that structure. Structures need the Spirit, but equally, the Spirit needs structures.

Now therefore we beg all clergy and people of the Episcopal Church of the USA to join us in our quest for spiritual renewal in every diocese and every parish through the outpouring of the Holy Spirit of God. Thankfully we recognize that God is moving in our midst already, and our purpose is to move with him. As witnesses to the renewing work of God, "we cannot but speak of what we have seen and heard" (Acts 4:20), and we cannot but commit ourselves to the ongoing quest for renewal in ever enriched and enriching forms. But we have no wish for isolation or separation from our brothers and sisters in Christ, either in our own Episcopal Church or in the world-wide Anglican Communion, and therefore it is our heartfelt prayer that we and those whom we represent will not find ourselves traveling alone.

> Pray for the peace of Jerusalem!
> "May they prosper who love you!
> Peace be within your walls
> and security within your towers!"
> For my brethren and companions' sake
> I will say, "Peace be within you!"
> For the sake of the House of the Lord our God,
> I will seek your good.   (Psalm 122:6–9)

APPENDIX III

PARTICIPANTS

THE 3 Rs CONFERENCE

The Rev. Keith Ackerman	Charleroi, Pennsylvania
The Rt. Rev. C. FitzSimmons Allison	Charleston, South Carolina
Ms. Isabel Anders	Shaker Heights, Ohio
The Rev. Carol Anderson	New York, New York
Mr. Robert M. Ayres, Jr.	Sewanee, Tennessee
The Rev. Frank Baltz	Smyrna, Georgia
The Rev. Stephen H. Bancroft	Lufkin, Texas
The Rev. John M. Barr, III	Mobile, Alabama
The Rev. James A. Basinger	Macon, Georgia
The Rev. Charles Bewick	Clayton, Missouri
Mr. Robert C. Bicknell	Nashua, New Hampshire
The Rev. Philip Bottomley	Sterling, Virginia
The Rev. Gregory O. Brewer	Winter Springs, Florida
Mr. Lee A. Buck	New Canaan, Connecticut
Mrs. Audrey Buck	New Canaan, Connecticut
The Rev. William J. Cavanaugh	San Antonio, Texas
The Rev. Charles Comella	Destin, Florida
The Rev. G. Patterson Connell	Cuero, Texas
The Rev. F. Brian Cox, IV	Newport Beach, California
The Rt. Rev. William J. Cox	Tulsa, Oklahoma
Mrs. Betty Cox	Tulsa, Oklahoma
The Rev. Sudduth Rea Cummings	San Antonio, Texas
Mrs. Charlotte Cummings	San Antonio, Texas
The Rev. M. Scott Davis	San Antonio, Texas
The Rev. Mike Flynn	Burbank, California
The Rt. Rev. William C. Frey	Denver, Colorado
The Rev. Everett L. Fullam	Darien, Connecticut
The Rev. Charles B. Fulton	Osprey, Florida

Mrs. Judith B. Fulton	Osprey, Florida
Mr. Harry C. Griffith	Winter Park, Florida
The Rev. John Guest	Sewickley, Pennsylvania
The Rev. Robert B. Hall	Live Oak, Florida
The Rev. James E. Hampson, Jr.	Huntingdon Valley, Pennsylvania
The Rev. Robert Haskell	Syracuse, New York
The Rt. Rev. Alden M. Hathaway	Pittsburgh, Pennsylvania
The Rev. Jay Haug	Jacksonville, Florida
The Rev. Whitey Haugan	Jacksonville, Florida
The Rev. Canon Derek Hawksbee	Union Mills, North Carolina
The Rev. William Hio	Schenectady, New York
Mrs. Akemi Hio	Schenectady, New York
The Rev. Canon John W. Howe	Fairfax, Virginia
The Rev. Philip E. Hughes	Rydal, Pennsylvania
The Rev. Robert D. Hughes, III	Sewanee, Tennessee
The Very Rev. Jack L. Iker	Sarasota, Florida
The Rev. Charles M. Irish	McLean, Virginia
The Rev. Stephen H. Jecko	Gainesville, Florida
Ms. Roberta L. Kenney	Seattle, Washington
The Rev. Richard Kew	Sewanee, Tennessee
The Rev. John P. Lambert	Bellevue, Washington
The Rev. David C. Lord	Vero Beach, Florida
Mrs. Julie C. Lord	Vero Beach, Florida
The Rt. Rev. Michael E. Marshall	Clayton, Missouri
The Rev. Kevin E. Martin	Seattle, Washington
Mrs. Sharon Martin	Seattle, Washington
The Rev. Peter Mason	Toronto, Ontario
The Rev. Dorsey McConnell	New Haven, Connecticut
Mr. Alan P. Medinger	Baltimore, Maryland
Mr. J. Keith Miller	Port Aransas, Texas
Andrea Wells Miller	Port Aransas, Texas
The Rev. William Millsaps	Sewanee, Tennessee
The Rev. Martyn Minns	Lafayette, Louisiana
The Rev. Gary Mitchener	Hanover, New Hampshire
The Rev. Forrest C. Mobley	Tallassee, Alabama
The Rev. Ian Montgomery	New Orleans, Louisiana
The Rev. Peter C. Moore	Greenwich, Connecticut
Mrs. Elaine Morgan	Oviedo, Florida
The Rev. Chuck Murphy	Birmingham, Alabama
Mrs. Anne Murphy	Birmingham, Alabama

Mr. David Neff	Downers Grove, Illinois
Ms. LaVonne Neff	Downers Grove, Illinois
The Rev. Wesley T. Nelson	Dallas, Texas
The Rev. Prof. J.I. Packer	Vancouver, British Columbia
The Rev. Sam Pascoe	Orange Park, Florida
Mrs. Beth Pascoe	Orange Park, Florida
The Rev. William T. Pickering	Pittsburgh, Pennsylvania
The Very Rev. Joel Pugh	Little Rock, Arkansas
The Rev. W. Graham Pulkingham	Aliquippa, Pennsylvania
The Rev. Marcus B. Robertson	Heflin, Alabama
The Rev. Fleming Rutledge	New York, New York
The Rev. Graham M. Smith	Lyndhurst, Ohio
The Rev. Steve Smith	Gainesville, Florida
Ms. Beth Spring	Washington, D.C.
Mr. James Sturm	Frankfort, Kentucky
Mrs. Ina Sturm	Frankfort, Kentucky
The Rev. George Stockhowe, Jr.	Virginia Beach, Virginia
The Rev. H. L. Thompson, III	Trumbull, Connecticut
The Rev. John R. Throop	Shaker Heights, Ohio
The Rev. Philip Turner	New York, New York
The Rev. John H. Vruwink	Medina, Washington
Mr. Paul M. Walter	Forest City, North Carolina
The Rev. Lewis Warren	Scottsbluff, Nebraska
The Rev. George F. Weld, II	Amherst, Virginia
The Rev. Todd H. Wetzel	Westlake, Ohio
Mr. Stephen S. Wilburn	Wilton, Connecticut
The Rev. John W. Yates, II	Falls Church, Virginia
The Rev. Paul F. M. Zahl	Scarborough, New York
The Rev. Philip Zampino	Libertytown, Maryland
Mrs. Jean Zampino	Libertytown, Maryland
The Rev. J. Robert Zimmerman	Lansdale, Pennsylvania